I0027831

Grass Roots Co-President's Campaign, Create 2,500,000 Disciples of America

Colonel Launeil Sanders

INMAN, SOUTH CAROLINA, USA

© 2006 by Dixie Press
All rights reserved.

ISBN 978-0-6151-5277-6
LCCN

Printed in the United States of America.

Preface

In 1990 my wife, Evelyn Ray Sanders, whom I had been married to for fifteen years was dying of liver cancer. Natalie Caroline Sanders, Aaron Neil Sanders, stepson Ronald Dale Franklin and I felt the Lord was eventually going to take her home to Heaven. I especially was not handling it very well. But here I am with my wife dying of liver cancer, and I felt they could not steal my two biological children in this freedom country of America. I was extremely naïve about America's legal system and man's law. But today, after some seventeen years of on-the-job-training in man's law, "America's legal system," I can truly testify to you today that man's law, America's legal system has absolutely nothing to do about truth, justice, honesty, fair play, righteousness and the Rule of Law! But it has all to do about infected, nefarious, profiteering, unscrupulous, dishonest attorneys who know the most polluted judge that can be manipulated, distorted and contaminated. I do not want you to misinterpret me as in my seventeen years in the Judiciary Wilderness, I have met only one Christian lawyer; his name is Matt Henderson who is a God Fearing American and Honorable Vietnam Veteran. I also will talk about him later in my book in his spiritual Vietnam testimony. For I realize there must be more than just one Christian lawyer in America, however God's path has me enduring others.

What this book is about is a vision, a dream to create 2,500,000 million disciples of America. Just as I asked all the students in Mrs. Ruth Pate's 'Journalism, Broadcast and News Class' at Dorman High School, Spartanburg, South Carolina, "Do you think a woman can become the First Woman President of America? And furthermore, is Hillary Clinton qualified to become the first woman president of America?" We all agreed! Many millions of God-fearing women live in the United States of America. They are all great citizens of America and are well qualified to become the first woman president of America. We all agreed Hillary Clinton is not a qualified candidate! Actually, Hillary is just another Rose law firm attorney who it is highly rumored to have had a fornicator, adulterer affair with Vincent Foster. For when Vincent Foster checked into the White House that last day, he never checked out. With all the sophistication and massive security measures at the White House, why did Vincent Foster never, ever properly security check out of the White House that day? It is a highly, 99.99% probability that Vincent Foster never, ever committed suicide, and that there are those still alive who really know what happened to Vincent Foster that fateful day. Hillary Clinton is fact fully married to a fornicator, adulterer Bill Clinton. "When Hillary and her fornicator, adulterer husband Bill Clinton were in power, they ordered the U.S. Internal Revenue Service Inc. to audit all whom they directed." For in November 1996, the day after Clinton and Gore were re-elected, Bill and Hillary

Clinton with their usual abuse of the government and power ordered the U.S. Internal Revenue Service to audit my 1994 and 1995 taxes. The U.S. IRS agent, Michael Woods, came out to my house, wrote down all the license plates on my vehicles in our driveway, came with no appointment, and was directly targeting me. I asked the IRS agent, Mr. Michael Woods, "Who ordered my tax audit?" Mr. Woods replied, "You must have really upset the highest, as POTUS ordered your tax audit!" Hillary Clinton is not, in my opinion, a God-fearing American qualified to be the next President of America. Thus, just as the Honorable late Reverend Jerry Falwell had an ABC law, I adopt the same "ABC Law," Anything But Clinton. I really don't believe God thinks it to be in the best interests of America for another Clinton in the White House.   For I wish to organize a "Grass Roots Co-President's Campaign and Create 2,500,000 Disciples of America." In September 2006 only about 74% of Americans trusted our 535 representatives in Washington, D.C. In October 2006 about three weeks before the National November 7, 2006, election, approximately 85% of Americans didn't trust our 535 representatives in Washington. Moreover, approximately 70% of Americans felt we should be out of Iraq and have our troops removed from Iraq! In addition, additionally, Hillary Clinton voted for the war and never admitted any mistakes. She does not favor the best interests of our troops. I truly believe all of the 300 million citizens of America will want to read my book. As if we stand together and God let's Jesus Christ walk with us in this grass roots effort, the Lord will guide us to achieve great things way greater than human items of the flesh! We do not certainly need more tainted attorneys in

America's government. Rather we need to weed out, shed America of unscrupulous lawyers. We need more American men and women who truly care about our Constitution, Declaration of Independence, and all our freedoms, liberties, and privileges that our ancestors framed for us! Thus, we plead and pray that if you are those untrustworthy attorneys, that you will repent, turn away from your acts of sin and accept Jesus Christ as your personal savior. America needs a New Industrial Revolution and an American revival. We need to reclaim our U.S. Constitution; we need to take back our government. We need to restore America's values to all families in America

Acknowledgements

My first and deepest thanks go to my God, my Personal Saviour, Jesus Christ, and to and my

profound faith that God answered my prayers and let my God walk with me in my trials and

tribulations. I am living in this earthly world today by the Grace of God! God has a plan for each of us

in this earthly world who have accepted Jesus Christ as our Personal Savior. I will always be grateful

to be a Child of God! In one of my substitute teaching assignments at Dorman High School, after I

mentioned that we are all Children of God, one of the students asked me if I were sure he was a Child

of God? I responded by saying to him, "Yes, I 'm sure you are a Child of God and that God and Jesus

Christ love you as the Holy Bible tells us exactly that. I am profoundly thankful that I am a Born

Again Christian and have publicly accepted Jesus Christ as my Personal Savior. Just as Moses was

required by God to remain over in the Desert Wilderness for forty years until he learned to 'Do it

God's Way", I am sincerely thankful that God has let Jesus Christ walk with me in my Faith. I am

thankful that God removed any and all obstacles in my trials that would hinder me from doing His

Will in His Plan for my Life. Someone told me to just "give up." That person did not have all the

details and did not know that God did not want me to give up! I have a credence that began with God,

v

"Everything I Do, I Do for the Glory, Power, and Glorification of God and my Savior, Jesus Christ." I owe a debt of Gratitude to my Loving God and to My Personal Savior, Jesus Christ, who is God's Holy Son whom God gave to us to save us all from our sin. Jesus Christ is the only perfect one in the Heaven and the world. Only Jesus Christ bore it all. Jesus Christ is the only one Risen From the Dead! Only by the Blood of Jesus Christ are we saved! I want to prepare myself each and and every moment in this earthly world for the second coming of Jesus Christ (that moment in the "twinkle of an eye.") The real key question for each of you who read my book is as follows: "In your personal opinion, how do you think you get to heaven?" Jot down the answer now, and when you finish the book, jot down your answer again.

My profound and sincere thanks are three-fold as mentioned above it is first to my God and my Personal Saviour, Jesus Christ, and to and my profound faith in God! Second, my thanks are to my Great Country of this United States of America. One of the reasons for writing this book is that I believe as God-fearing God wants us to assemble together, Stand in the Gap for Jesus Christ, Tarry with our God, and reclaim our government back from those who have hijacked it. God does not want us to stay on the sidelines. He, God, wants us to "Mount up with Wings as Eagles and restore Our Godly Heritage to Our Beloved Godly Founded Country!" I am thankful to be a Natural Born American Citizen.I have strict oath of allegiance to our Great United States of America. In my 17 years over in this Judiciary Wilderness, I believe if some of Our Founding Forefathers could be risen from the dead as Christ, they might vomit all over some who have stomped all over our United States Constitution! I am thankful that God has blessed America. Just as the first time my wife sat foot on America's soil, she stated "America is a Great Freedom Country and has many Churches." My wife, Janneth Sanders, is a proud U.S. Naturalized American Citizen sworn in her Oath of Allegiance to the Great United States of America on June 5, 1998, along with 81 other immigrants.

My third deepest, grateful, profound thanks go to my God-fearing family that God has blessed! My life time partner and wife is Janneth Sanders. I tell her every day, "I Can Not Do without Her."

God had Janneth praying for me in the 1990's way before God guided this devout Christian lady into my God-fearing life. God brought me a Christian lady from over 15,000 miles, half way around this earthly world, to share the rest of this earthly life! I want to express my deepest gratitude and thanks to my God for blessing Janneth and me with our two children who are both gifts from God. In this earthly world, we all Born Again Christians know all of our "children are gifts from God!" The Holy Bible tells us in His Holy word. Our two gifts from God are our daughter, Dorothy Love Sanders, and our son, Colonel Tony Sanders. I am also very thankful and grateful for God's gifts of the children that God blessed Evelyn and me before she died of primary liver cancer at an early age of forty. Our two children are daughter, Natalie Caroline Sanders and son, Aaron Neil Sanders. God also blessed Evelyn with a son from her first marriage, Ronald Dale Franklin, who I pray God will fill his heart with the "Fruit of the Spirit" in the coming moments. Yes, the "Fruit of the Spirit" is the Holy Spirit which reigns in each of our hearts who have given our lives to Christ!

My deepest and profound thanks also go to Pastor Hank Williams, Chief Pastor for Boiling Springs First Baptist Church, for his preaching and delivery of God's Word last May 2006. Pastor Hank Williams delivered several sermons from Galatians on the "Fruit of the Spirit," which is the Holy Spirit which lives in each of our hearts who have accepted Christ as our Personal Savior. Pastor Hank Williams, I will always be grateful that God guided you and all our Brothers and Sisters in Christ at Boiling Springs First Baptist Church into Janneth's and my life. I was totally inspired by the "Fruit of the Spirit" of our living Christ to finish this book I had originally started back in 1999.

I am also want to thank Johnaca Dunlap and Teresa Dees of the University of South Carolina Upstate, Spartanburg, South Carolina, for their courteous help, generosity, graciousness, and skills in assisting me in the formatting, images and other computer skills enabling me to finish the book. Not being as proficient in computer skills, my deepest thanks go to Johnaca Dunlap and Teresa Dees for their patience, expertise and encouragement in finishing the final product.

I also want to thank *Blue Ridge Broadcasting, WMIT 106.9 FM,* Christian radio station located in Black Mountain, North Carolina. Janneth's and my car radios have been tuned to this station for the past thirteen years. They provide a God-fearing Christian service to the several states area. Their Christian hymns and other programming are excellent. Two of the artists who may be heard often are *Casting Crowns* and *Mercy Me*. Two of their songs respectfully are "Voice of Truth" by *Casting Crowns* and "Bring the Rain" by *Mercy Me*. *"If God lets Jesus Christ walk with us in this grass roots political movement,* everything is accomplishable, no Exceptions." Everything is achievable through Christ. When we get through the primaries, we hope both groups will be with us along with other singing groups to celebrate Sup with the Lord on the Washington Mall!

ABOUT THE AUTHOR

This book, 'Grass Roots Co-President's Campaign; Create 2,500,000 Disciples of America,' is about reclaiming our government, our Constitution, which has been hijacked by politicians and lobbyists. This is about creating 50,000 Disciples per state in a grass roots campaign movement in 2007 and 2008. This movement will have a God-fearing man and a God-fearing woman running together as President and Vice-President and participating in the fifteen months campaign and debates together. In the book, Colonel Sanders demonstrates that through leadership that gasoline prices will immediately be reduced to $1.00 per gallon after January 20, 2009. For nearly twenty years, Colonel Sanders has fought a corrupt legal and judicial system, seeking justice under Constitutional Law! Having experienced the fallen state of the state, he lays out a vigorous and God-centered approval to reclaiming our inalienable rights as promised by our Constitution by refocusing on the Creator as the final source of all Law.

It is so essential in America for us to stand in the gap for Jesus and take our government back from those tainted individuals who have stomped on our Constitution. Many have died for and given all for this great country. Colonel Sanders prays they should not be ignored! Colonel Sanders' wife died of liver cancer in 1990, this book is really about the past 17 years of his life in his trials and tribulations in our country's state courts, U.S. Federal District Courts, U.S. Federal Appellate Circuit Courts and the U.S. Supreme Court in demonstrating that America's Legal System is totally broken. Colonel Sanders has a vision, as was the case in 2006, that 84% of America didn't trust their 535 representatives in Washington, D.C. He believes that this movement, "Grass Roots Co-President's Campaign and Create 2,500,000 Disciples of America," is a spiritual solution to a societal problem. Without the input and blessings of God Almighty, this cannot be called 'One Nation Under God.' If we are to survive as a people, we must return to the Founding Fathers' vision of the Constitutional Republic.

Attached below is Colonel Launeil Sanders' resume and credentials:

He is a 27 years chemical and environmental international professional. He was the "Only Environmental Candidate" for Congress for the U.S. Federal 4th Congressional District of South Carolina in 1998. Colonel Sanders has a Bachelor of Science in Engineering Chemistry from Christian Brothers University, Memphis, Tennessee; and completed 90% of his Master of Science in Civil Engineering with Environmental Engineering as a major from Memphis State University. He has published the following articles: (1) Prepared for EPA's Office of Solid Waste a listing of all hazardous waste operators under Resource Conservation and Recovery Act (RCRA) Incinerators, Subpart O; and published technical paper in Chemical Engineering Progress,, March 1983, titled "Compilation of Hazardous Waste Manufacturers and Operators" (2) Presented and published "Detailed Scope of Work for Consolidated Incineration Facility at installed cost of $70,000,000 for Savannah River Nuclear Plant," presented at International Incineration Conference of Low Level Radioactive and Hazardous Wastes, Knoxville, Tennessee, May 1989. He possesses a Secret "Q" Security Clearance with the United States Department of Energy at Savannah River Nuclear Plant, Aiken, South Carolina.

Colonel Sanders has pending a Utility Wastewater Process Patent before the U.S. Patent and Trademark Office that will save all the 850 U.S. pulp and paper mills ten billion dollars of electricity annually and clean up a toxic, hazardous wastewater! The pulp and paper mills' wastewater is black as your shoe! There is currently a criminal loop hole that allows all the 850 mills to discharge into our streams and rivers a toxic, hazardous wastewater. My patent cures the problem and dynamically improves the environment for all Americans. He has served as a technical advisory panel member for the Solar Energy Research Institute (SERI), U.S. Department of Energy and U.S. Environmental Protection Agency on biomass gasification.

He has designed nerve gas, hazardous wastes incineration complexes both for the U.S. Army Corps. of Engineers and the U.S. Department of Energy at Savannah River Plant. Colonel Sanders has served in different management capacities for Boise Cascade and Agrico Chemical Company in manufacturing. Additionally, he has other fourteen years of architectural and engineering construction experience with various firms including Raytheon Engineers and Constructors Inc., Fluor Daniel Inc., C.T. Main Inc. (subsidiary of Parsons Corporation), Rust International and "think tank" Mitre Corporation. He also has governmental environmental engineering experience with the U.S. Environmental Protection Agency and South Carolina Department of Health and Environmental Control.

Contents

1

EVELYN DIES

Moreover, in a Brief Executive Summary, my wife Evelyn had four sisters and two brothers. Georgia West and my spouse, Evelyn Sanders, were two of the five sisters born to Robert Ray and their Mother Mrs. Willie Ray. There were tremendous amounts of domestic violence in their household and upbringing. As the Father, Robert Ray and Mother, Mrs. Willie Ray participated in knock down drag out battles. Robert Ray was an alcoholic and Mrs. Willie Ray became an alcoholic. When Mrs. Willie Ray vacationed with us in 1980, she drank almost ¾ of a fifth of vodka a day. Georgia West nor my spouse Evelyn Sanders nor the other three sisters ever visited or spoke to their earthly Father in the last thirty years of his life. Robert Ray died in 1982.

I went to meet and visit their earthly Father, Robert Ray, on at least four occasions before he died in Maiden, North Carolina, in 1982. I went with the two Brothers who had that "agape Love for their earthly father just as I believe they had for their Heavenly Father." The two brothers were Sonny Ray and Robert Ray Jr. "I believe Sonny Ray has been called on to be with our Heavenly Father." If you live on or in this earthly world with as much hatred of Satan as these five sisters possessed, or that the devil possessed them in their hearts, you cannot know the "Fruit of The Spirit." The "Fruit of the Spirit" is the Holy Spirit which lives in each of our hearts who are born again and accept Jesus Christ as our Personal Savior. Only through the Blood of Christ, as Jesus Christ is the only one who has been risen from the dead! Jesus Christ is Lord, the Messiah, Son of David, the King of all Kings, and the Holy Spirit, the "Fruit of the Spirit" that lives in each of us who have been born again!

That morning I had called my friend and associate, Dale Hopkins, who had been my boss at Charles T. Main (Subsidiary of Parsons Corporation) in Charlotte, North Carolina. Dale and I worked for said company from February 1985 to April 1990. Dale had went with me to visit Evelyn {over at this sister in law, Mrs. Emil Parker, in Davidson, North Carolina, in October 26, 1990, that Thursday evening. I had gotten a Mecklenburg County, North Carolina, Superior Court Judge, Honorable Robert Johnston, to issue a Temporary Restraining Order giving me permission to visit with my spouse of 15 years, the Evelyn Ray Franklin Sanders. As you will later discover, I, Launeil Sanders had two sisters in law who sabotaged my life. One of these sisters in law was the one and only Georgia West of Gastonia, North Carolina. Georgia West was a cop for the City of Gastonia, North Carolina. However, I never felt that here in America could someone criminally kidnap your two children, remove them from South Carolina, take them across state lines to North Carolina, and on July 25, 1990, and obtain an illegal custody order. The attorney who aided Georgia West was "the one and only James Carpenter of Carpenter & James attorney firm." Then, for her and her attorney, James Carpenter, both to get Gaston County District Judge Catherine Stevens, who was both friends of Georgia West and James Carpenter, to obtain a custody order from both Evelyn and me, the biological parents, was unthinkable. However, Georgia West, a cop for the City of Gastonia, North Carolina, on that day July 25, 1990, obtained an Emergency Custody Order, case # 90-CVD-2566. Pursuant to the North Carolina Law, Evelyn and I were via the North Carolina law required to be given three days to respond to any North Carolina emergency custody order. However, many of the officers of the Gaston

Court perpetrated racketeering. Georgia West did sue Evelyn Sanders and Launeil Sanders, and she was able to get signed an Emergency Custody Order from Stevens. Stevens signed the Emergency Custody Order. The Order was on James Carpenter's law firm stationary "Carpenter and James!"

Thus, this Thursday, November 29, 1990, I had asked Dale Hopkins to accompany me over to Davidson, North Carolina, to visit Evelyn that evening. Around 3:30 P. M. that afternoon, Dale Hopkins called me. We both were now working for Fluor Daniel Engineers and Constructors in Greenville, South Carolina. Dale said to me "Neil, I just talked to Mr. Emil Parker at their Davidson, North Carolina, home, and he told me that your wife, Evelyn, passed away today!" The first thing I did after I had gotten off the phone from Dale was to call up to Georgia West's house. I got Georgia West on the phone. I immediately asked, "How are Natalie and Aaron doing?" She responded by saying, "They are doing fine, but it is none of your "g*^&@*$N business!"

Immediately I slammed the phone against the wall in my office, and a few seconds afterward, I looked to see if I had broken my Fluor Daniel office phone. Our offices in the Fluor Daniel "Black Darfader building" were really partitions. One of my engineer associates, Mark Sapeda, heard me slam the phone and came over to ask and incur of what the problem(s) were. I told him that my spouse, Evelyn, passed away today. I also told him that this sister in law, Georgia West, refused to let me talk with my two children.

I do not remember what sequences of events occurred next and do not remember going home to 4729 Worden Drive, Spartanburg, South Carolina, later. That evening I remember calling my Mother and stepfather, Harold, in Atoka, Tennessee. I told them Evelyn passed away today, November 29, 1990. You know, I knew what I was up against when Georgia West kidnapped my children six months earlier to Evelyn dying (this happened on July 25, 1990). However, I was too naïve. With my wife dying of liver cancer, I didn't think she could steal my two biological children.

Wherefore, the truth is if when you go up against depraved officers of the Court, Georgia West and her contaminated Gastonia counsel (James Carpenter); and who both are cozy little personal friends of the District Judge Catherine Stevens, then they can do anything they wish! Catherine Stevens, who was a stupid, inept attorney who could not make it, was encouraged by James Carpenter and Gastonia attorney Locke Bell to run for Gaston District Judge. By gosh she ran for Gaston District Judge. She was successful in the election. That is how defiled the Gaston County, North Carolina, legal system is! Therefore, if you or any of your loved ones get detained in Gaston County, send entire emergency aide that you have available to you and pray constantly.

I thought that I would have some power and edge in getting my children back now that Evelyn had died. However, I was soon to learn that the premise discussed in preceding paragraph reigns in power. If you have the exploiting, underhanded lawyer, the venal Catherine Stevens, and the decayed Gaston Law on your side and all, of which, are officers of the Court, you can do anything you wish. {Gaston County, North Carolina, is the same place, where the group of six to a dozen Gaston County Sheriffs' deputies and Gaston City police, in or around 1991 and 1992 poured cooking oil and human urine over the homeless people. It took Charlotte civil rights attorney, James Ferguson, to file a civil rights suit and get some form of justice for these homeless people.} The moral is if you or anyone of your loved ones are detained in Gaston County, North Carolina, pray a lot for you are up against a lot of triple deviate individuals who are all part of and are officers of the Court.

Now it is Friday, November 30, 1990, day after Evelyn died. I got up early to go to Lincolnton, North Carolina. I went to view Evelyn's body and to check on funeral arrangements. {For background, I should point out I was robbed in a Hardee's restaurant in 1983, which will detail why I had since carried my firearm! In December 26, 1983, in Birmingham, Alabama, the night after `Christmas I went into the airport road Hardee's. It was being robbed by two black Birmingham-

4

Americans and they were committing criminal acts for their 4th time. These two were convicted three times of armed robbery. This was prior to any three strikes law. Before this Hardee's robbery, I had never owned a pistol or gun. Nevertheless, after the robbery, my cousin, who was a Memphis police officer, recommended a Memphis licensed gun shop. I purchased a 357 magnum and a five-shooter 38 caliper.}

Thus, I had since 1984 carried either the 357-magnum pistol or the thirty eight-caliper firearms with me. In the Hardee's robbery, that December 26, 1983, the criminal who cocked the thirty eight-caliper firearm and threatened to kill me was Reginald Green. Reginald Green had three prior convictions for armed robbery. That night when he jumped across the counter and shouted a profanity at me, "mf, if you don't come around here and get in freezer, I'm going to blow your mf head off!" I knew this was the real thing; this wasn't HBO, Showtime, or any other movie. The Birmingham police let us out of freezer some fifty minutes later. In addition, you know, today, thank God for the God-Fearing Americans like the American Rifle Association, as they stand for values, principles for which our forefathers fled Europe and drew up our Constitution. I find it paradoxical that people think we have freedoms! All those freedoms have been gradually taken away; they have been destroyed! If we do not act and stand for the principles, which our forefathers stood for in drafting the Constitution, our government will continually be run by the filthy, wealthy, ultra rich and ultra filthy rich $3000 per hour lobbyists and other politicians, who do actually run our Government. "God, Please Bless all the God-fearing Americans who have the faith in Almighty God, walk with Jesus Christ, and have the Holy Devine Spirit reign inside them!" For as God was putting me through these trials and tribulations, and just as Moses was sentenced to the Wilderness for forty years until he learned to "do it God's way," God has assigned me to these trials. Moreover, God knew that I had not yet learned to do it God's way! Yes, even though a fornicator, adulterer, cop Georgia West had no legal right to sue

Evelyn and me for our two biological children, it happened. The breakdown of the moral values in this great country is due to taking God out of our Heritage. God has been thrown out of our schools, the Bible has been taken out of our schools and the prayer has been thrown into the toilet! When I ran for Congress in the U.S. 4th Congressional District in 1998 (as you will read in future chapters) I had an interview in Columbia, South Carolina, with a well-known radio station. Ten minutes into the interview, I told him I stood for school prayer. He cancelled the rest of my interview. It was supposed to be a thirty minutes interview! Praise God as Reginald Green or the other armed robber in the Birmingham robbery evidently had never met God nor accepted Jesus Christ. This also applies to all the school shooters and college shooters! Praise God for Honorable Judge Roy Moore in Alabama, who was persecuted and lost his job. He stood in the gap and stood for faith in God! May Jesus Christ continue to walk with you Judge Roy Moore.

Thus, I got up to Lincolnton, North Carolina, that morning, about 9:30 A.M. on Friday, November 30, 1990. I first went to Nations Bank (then it was NCNB North Carolina). Since then, Nations Bank merged with Bank America. There, at the bank, I got a notarized document requesting in written format and Notary Sealed that I was requesting of Drum's Funeral Home, Lincolnton, North Carolina, to perform an autopsy of my deceased spouse, Evelyn Sanders. I had some proof that the two sisters in law had conspired and had possibly given her a lethal dose of morphine. Evelyn committed suicide, assisted by the two sisters in law. As Mrs. Emil Parker on July 10, 1990, at her Davidson, North Carolina, home where she was keeping Evelyn stated, "Well, Evelyn has suffered enough and she should be allowed to have her wish, allowed to die!" Well, I was depressed, but I knew as long as Evelyn had the desire to live, help Aaron with his homework and be with Natalie, she had the will to live. However, here, I have two sinful sisters in law, who convinced Evelyn that it was time for her to die. They seemed to believe that she had suffered too much. I know they convinced her to just give up and die! Of course, I was lost out there, and even though Aaron, Natalie, and I knew Evelyn was eventually going to die of the liver cancer, I was not handling it very well.

Thus, somewhere around 10 A.M. that November 30, 1990, I delivered the notarized autopsy request to Drum's funeral home and chatted with the director. I can not remember his name, maybe Scott, something like that. Then I called my attorney, Daniel Clifton, in Charlotte and asked him if I did or did not have legal rights to get an autopsy performed on my dead spouse. Dan Clifton said I did have that right. I drove over to Davidson, North Carolina, to talk with the police chief. I met personally with the City of Davidson, North Carolina, chief. He told me that Mecklenburg County would not pay for the autopsy, but that Lincoln County Medical Examiner (Lincoln County Hospital) could perform the autopsy at my personal expense. Thus, I drove back to Lincolnton, North Carolina, and went to Lincoln County Memorial Hospital. I arranged for about $1000 to have autopsy performed on Evelyn. I then left the hospital to drive back over to relay this information to Drum's funeral home.

It was now around 3 o'clock P.M. in the afternoon on this Friday November 30, 1990, and I was driving from the hospital back over to Drum's Funeral Home. Police Chief, Terry Burgin stopped me. I knew Terry Burgin. I also knew that he was a very close friend of my sister in law. As I mentioned, I always took my 38-caliper pistol with me. In North Carolina, the gun has to be in open, and it was on the dash. In South Carolina, the law is different. The gun has to be concealed. Of course, if I had been thinking clearly, I should have left the gun in Spartanburg, South Carolina. Well, it was already conspired that this little Terry Burgin would arrest me, and he did. Yes, I was arrested by Terry Burgin, kept in jail and prohibited from seeing my dead spouse's body and attending her funeral. I had been married to Evelyn fifteen years, and now in America was being prohibited from viewing my deceased spouse's body at the funeral home. I was charged with improper concealment of my pistol weapon; however, this was a bogus, criminal conspiracy of Terry Burgin. After Evelyn's funeral, I was let released from jail. They gave me a Court date for December 11, 1990. One thing that Terry Burgin said to me in the police car on that November 30, 1990, I will never, ever release! "Well, you haven't got to view your wife's body yet, have you?" I know revenge is with the Lord; and that day, that November 30, 1990, I want you to know I felt Terry Burgin was the lowest life human being that had ever lived in Lincolnton, North Carolina, and America! I did not know how lost I was, or why God was choosing me. I was still continuing to put my faith in man's law. I did not understand how lost I was, and I knew Georgia West had more power, authority and prestige than me. I knew man's law in Gaston County had nailed me again. Nevertheless, of course, only Jesus Christ, the Son of God, endured all the pain to be crucified, dead, and buried; and the third day arose again from the dead. For Jesus Christ had criminal fabricated charges raised and charged against Him! The priests and others had fabricated criminal charges against Jesus Christ consisting of (1) preaching to overthrow the Roman Rule; (2) preaching to overthrow the government by preaching to reject your taxes and not pay the government your taxes; and (3) that Jesus was claiming to be "King of Kings." In addition, the third charge was the only one that was the genuine truth! For only through the divine blood of Christ are we all saved! Only by the grace of God, am I living in this earthly world today at the time of this writing. But only if you publicly accept Christ as your Personal Savior, repent, turn away from your life of sin, and trust in Christ as your new walk in Christ, can you have divine spiritual eternal life.

I should point out as you are going to see in Chapter 2 upcoming where Georgia West knew she had me beat, and she knew she could whip me in her bias, prejudiced Gaston County legal system. For Gaston County never, ever had legal jurisdiction as neither I, Evelyn nor our two children had ever lived in Gaston County. We had lived in Lincolnton, North Carolina 28092, Lincoln County, from September 1983 until July 1990 until we moved to South

Carolina. For when she got this child custody Emergency Order signed on July, 25, 1990, (case # 90-CVD-2566, six months before Evelyn died), {as I, Launeil Sanders, was out of town when she performed these illegal acts} she was shacking-up with fornicator, adulterer, Jim Anderson, who was still married to his wife Judy Anderson!} In addition, I later talked and met Judy Anderson to see if she would come into Gaston Court to help me win back custody of my two children. She said, "all the Gaston legal system was corrupt, and that Georgia West and Jim Andersen deserved each other. She would not help me." She referred me to another source who told me that Georgia West had hopped in the back seat of the patrol cars with Jim Andersen and others and had been nick named "Backseat West" by Gaston police officer Jeanette Seagel. And also, Georgia West at her Cherryville, North Carolina home where she and Jim were fornicating, shacking-up, adulterating up, she also had her oldest son Issac West with his live-in girlfriend and their illegitimate baby which had been born one month prior in June 1990. Just as the Atlanta murderer Mark Barton who killed nine persons at an Atlanta brokerage day traders on July 29, 1999, and killed his second wife and two children earlier, God is in Control. God is the Absolute Law, the only genuine law! God's Law is absolute and the only law, which is not flawed! As only God knows what is in Georgia West's heart, I can only state how I was treated, "inhuman." I am a born again Christian, and in all my trials and tribulations since 1990 I have never, ever blamed God! I really know revenge is with the Lord, and realistically I am absent of any hate and anger. I am only trying to express how I really felt those days back in July 25, 1990. How can an Aunt, Georgia West, sue Launeil Sanders and Evelyn Sanders, husband and wife, in Gaston County, North Carolina, where we had never ever resided? We had lived in Lincoln County, North Carolina, Lincolnton, North Carolina, from 1983 until 1990. Gaston County never, ever had jurisdiction over, Evelyn, Natalie, or son Aaron and me. However, fear not, Catherine Stevens had just

9

sentenced Aaron Sanders and Natalie Sanders to live in fornication and adultery and more worshipping of the flesh. Now in 2006, my daughter Natalie has had two abortions. Why should I not feel that Catherine Stevens and the North Carolina legal system violated theirs and my civil rights and sentenced them to death? Catherine Stevens surely had in that July 25, 1990, sentenced Natalie and Aaron to death. In the Bible, Romans 6:23 "For the wages of sin is death; the gift of God is eternal life through Jesus Christ our Lord." The gift of God: Sanctification of life does not earn eternal life; it is still God's gracious gift.

Well, I went back to Lincoln County Court on December 11, 1990. The Judge delivered that I was innocent of the firearms charge. However, the "big picture" was that certain specific agents had kept me from viewing my wife's body and going to her funeral! Nick Batounis of Lincolnton, North Carolina, told me afterwards that Terry Burgin told him and another neighbor "that they were going to keep me away from the Saturday, December 1, 1990, funeral." Evelyn Sanders was my spouse for fifteen years.

It is difficult to get to the truth in America's Man courts. The system manifests itself about vitiated attorneys who play the criminal dirty lawyer tricks to win. It is not about truth and justice or the rule of law. I'm still trying to learn the path God has designed for me and to continually learn every day of my life to do it God's way! <u>But in one of my recent daily communions with my Lord, he told me it was in His Holy Plan that I would lose control of my biological children.</u> God Bless America! I have never ever blamed God for my trials and tribulations; I have always kept my faith. I thanked God for communicating this to me in my daily communion with Him!

2

SABOTAGE OF MY LIFE BY TWO SISTER-IN-LAWS

That I had accepted an Environmental Engineer position with Fluor Daniel Engineers and Constructors in Greenville, South Carolina, on April 1, 1990. I desired industrial work, and I had an alcoholic, cocaine drug addict stepson named Ronald Dale Franklin, who I wanted to finally get out on his own. Ronnie would not be moving to Spartanburg, South Carolina, with us. The indecent deeds by this stepson were devastating. He was a cocaine drug addict. He would steal everything he could get his hands on. He really did not give a royal care about his Mother. His alcohol and drug habits were more important to him than his own Mother! I had bought him two cars. I had loved him as his Father. He never paid a cent, never paid any insurance, and never helped his Mother. About the only capabilities, that he did possess was the stealing of his Mother's credit cards out of her billfold and running up large sums of gasoline bills and other bills with his drug addicts' friends.

On or approximately May 23, 1990, while I was in Philadelphia, Pennsylvania, on a Dupont job for Fluor Daniel, one sister in law, Mrs. Emil Parker and the other sister in law, Georgia West, moved Evelyn over to Mrs. Parker's home in Pine Street, Davidson, North Carolina. Mrs. Emil Parker came back to get the electric medical bed I had bought Evelyn. I realize now that I should have had more hindsight; however, I did not. I should have hired a full-time nurse, or that we should have moved back to Atoka, Tennessee, and lived close to my Mother. I made some critical mistakes. God let me make these choices during these terminal times. I have zero domestic disputes against me, and furthermore, they had no legal right to move my wife out of our house. I had never hit my wife or my two children. God knew that I was trusting in man's law too much. Just as God left Moses over in the other side of the desert for forty years, God knew that I had to sacrifice my life in the body of Christ. In the Bible, Romans 12:1 "I beseech you therefore, brethren, by the mercies of God, that ye present your bodies a living sacrifice, holy, acceptable unto God, which is your reasonable service." *Brethren-* this appeal for dedication of life is addressed to believers (as also in 1 Corinthians 6:20; James 4:7). *By the mercies of God-* which has been described in the preceding chapters. *Present-* A decisive decision as in Romans 6:13. *living sacrifice-* in contrast to dead animal sacrifices. *reasonable service-* intelligent, rational, and deliberate.

He knew I had to be broken! He knew I had to learn the basics: "Everything I do, I do for the power and glory of Christ." However, I did not at that specific time of my life. Now, I am a born again Christian! I realize that the most important thing in this earthly world is to publicly accept Jesus Christ as my personal savior, repent, turn away from my life of sin, and to trust God. To be anew in Christ and be obedient to God is what it is all about in this earthly world. For just as my wife, Janneth, has told me many times "you can do nothing without the Lord." Another most precious, loving kind credence that my spouse now, Janneth Emberador Sanders, told me in 1993 is my Credence, "Launeil, I just wanted you to know that love is an experience that began with God, fulfilled through our Personal Savior Jesus Christ, nurtured within me and I share with you!" You know my wife shared the

Christian Love with me. As I know that Janneth and I share "agape love," the true Christian love that initiated with God and came from God. My wife now, Janneth Emberador Sanders, said one evening after my Mother was starved to death, drugged to death in an institution in Tennessee in July 11, 2004; that she had a vision that Mother came into our bedroom and said to her in the vision, "Don't worry, Janneth, I'm in Heaven!" Shown on the following page is photograph 1, Natalie Caroline Sanders and Aaron Neil Sanders, our two biological children God granted Evelyn and me. Photograph 2- shows Son Aaron Sanders and his wife Allison; Bottom photo, from left Janneth Sanders, Aaron Sanders, wife Allison holding our daughter Dorothy Love Sanders; Shown is a group photograph 3, Evelyn, me, Launeil, Natalie, Ronnie and Aaron in the top left insert.

Everything I did was to trust in man's Law. I could not accept that my two children were lost here in this earthly world. I should have renewed my faith. However, I did not. I thought man's law was eventually going to work for me as the law was on my side. I kept coming up against triple crooked officers of the court in their home turf. Additionally, I was so naïve of America's judicial system. However, in 2006 some fifteen lawsuits later, I am well aware of what America's judicial system consists, and how it works! That it has nothing to do about truth and justice. If at this time I had been a more controlled, born-again Christian, I would have always known that you can achieve nothing unless the Lord walks with you. I had let my life back slide with the devil getting more priority. Just as God has a plan for all of us, we are all sinners saved by the Blood of Christ. God gave Jesus Christ to save us from our sins. To live is Christ and to die is gain, from Philippians 1: 21.

I know God allows us all to make our choices, and I was a Christian who had had the largest backslide in this earthly World. I did not trust as much in God's Law, which is what I should have been doing! Again, as mentioned earlier, I knew I was enduring a lot of trials and tribulations. However, I never, ever blamed God for these trials. I knew better. I eventually committed myself to sacrifice my life in the body of Christ. I wanted to learn to do it God's way, to strive to ask God to bring a Christian Lady in my earthly life, and to go have some of God's children in our Christian lives, if it were God's blessing (as all of our children are gifts from God). I joined a Christian club, and God brought Janneth Emberador into my life. I wanted to learn to do it God's way, as that is what it's really about in this earthly world. Every week now from the time Mrs. Emil Parker moved Evelyn over to her home in Davidson, North Carolina, on May 23, 1990, my life was starting to spiral into non-recovery until December 1992 when God guided Janneth into my life {future chapters}. At Fluor Daniel, I was working on a Dupont job. It required me to catch a plane in Charlotte on Sunday evenings and return on Thursday evenings. Thus, I dropped Aaron and Natalie off at Georgia West's in Cherryville, North Carolina, and paid her weekly for seeing after them. In July 6, 1990, my mother and stepfather, Harold Craig, my brother Larry and his wife Faye came from Tennessee to help us move to Spartanburg to our new house at 4729 Worden Drive, Spartanburg, South Carolina. So Aaron, Natalie, and I moved to our new house in Spartanburg on that Saturday, July 6, 1990, with Mother, Harold, and brother and his wife's help. On Friday, July 5, 1990, Aaron and I had come to the Spartanburg law offices of Lawrence and Lawrence to close on the house at 4729 Worden Drive, Spartanburg, South Carolina. Natalie was at a Girl Scout church camp for the entire week.

Three weeks later Georgia West took them from our new home to visit their Mother who was at Mrs. Parker's house in Davidson, North Carolina. She, Georgia West had already conspired and prepared a criminal plan. As on July 25, 1990, when I was out of town, she got this "Emergency Custody Order, Case # 90-CVD-2566", Gaston County District Court, filed on July 25, 1990, by her attorney James Carpenter of Carpenter & James law firm. James Carpenter drafted this order on his company stationery "Carpenter & James". And another little triple profligate buddy, Catherine Stevens, signed that Order on that July 25, 1990. I later filed a written formal complaint to the North

14

Carolina Judicial Standards Commission; however, I quickly found out that the Commission and the North Carolina Bar Grievance Committee were simply figurehead agencies to give all citizens a 'good like feeling.' They never intended to help, nor have they ever sanctioned any attorneys or judges in North Carolina. This Durham North Carolina District Attorney, Mr. Nifong, whom it seems and the evidence directly points that he has committed severe criminal racketeering and criminal prosecutorial misconduct and malicious prosecution (at the time of this writing in January 2007), probably won't be disbarred or prosecuted. Rather since this is in North Carolina, he probably will not even get a slap on the wrist! In addition, probably so few North Carolina attorneys have ever been sanctioned, you could start at one and over-shoot the actual number. I should point out that later I will discuss in detail that Evelyn, I, Natalie, and Aaron never, ever lived in Gaston County, North Carolina. That we had lived at our permanent residence, 215 North Oak Street, Lincolnton, North Carolina, 28092, Lincoln County, from September 1983 until July 1990. Gaston County never, ever had legal jurisdiction; jurisdiction was always with Lincoln County, North Carolina, or South Carolina.

Earlier, after Mother and Harold finished getting us moved in to our Spartanburg new house in Oak Forest, they stayed until July 13, 1990. We all went to visit Evelyn at Davidson, North Carolina, at the Parkers' house on July 10, 1990. At this time just a couple of weeks before Georgia West got this custody order, I should have been more alert. In reality, I never underestimated Georgia West; however, I still was very naive about America's judicial system. As in a free America, I felt there was no way she could steal my biological children. Nevertheless, you will see the ("Emergency Custody Order, Case # 90-CVD-2566" signed by Catherine Stevens) ruled superior and reigned supremacy! When you have wicked officers of the Court on the opposing side, they can do anything they want to! Neither my spouse nor I or my two children ever lived in Gaston County, North Carolina. They never, ever had jurisdiction. We, always, from 1983 to that day in July 6, 1990, lived in Lincolnton, North Carolina, Lincoln County. Jurisdiction was always with Lincoln County. Nevertheless, you see the first premise stated earlier, "If you are part of the fraudulent County Officers of the Court and the North Carolina State law, you can do anything you want." This was exactly what has happened in the "Duke Lacrosse case" as three Duke College students have been falsely accused prosecuted and had their lives and their families' lives criminally destroyed! Additionally, pursuant to North Carolina law this was criminally illegal; and that also pursuant to the state law, Evelyn Sanders and Launeil Sanders were to be given three days to respond to any Emergency Custody Order. However, those rights were jammed down our throats. If you go up against decayed, adulterated officers of the court, who commit civil and potential criminal racketeering, it does not matter! Even if you have 1000 attorneys representing you, it is rigged, framed against you!

18

3

WHOLE FAILURE OF ENTIRE NORTH CAROLINA JUDICIAL SYSTEM AS IT FAILED TO PROTECT MY SPOUSE EVELYN

In August 1990 I filed a "Petition for Appointment of a Guardian Ad Litem" for my spouse Evelyn Sanders in the Lincoln County, North Carolina, the City of Lincolnton, North Carolina. However, I was told since she was now living in Davidson, North Carolina, and since she was in Mecklenburg County, I would have to repetition in Charlotte, North Carolina, the seat of Mecklenburg County. I did file repetition. A hearing was scheduled and held on September 17, 1990, at the Probate Clerk of Mecklenburg County in Charlotte. The fact that Evelyn Sanders was dying of liver cancer, was a morphine addict, was on other tremendous dosages of other dangerous drugs such as Prozac, Ativan, Morphine Liquid, Morphine Sulphate Contin, Dieldran, and other toxic tranquilizers was very, very important. I knew the State of North Carolina had a legal responsibility under the North Carolina law to protect Evelyn from these two sisters in law and other evil agents. However, the state did not! Evelyn did not appear at the September 17, 1990, Guardian Ad Litem hearing; and of course, the North Carolina refused to protect her.

One of the recent political advertisements for one of the Republicans running for the U.S Senate here in South Carolina recently ran an advertisement that he did not know where Love began! Well just as I stated earlier, it is with God. My fiancée and I, as stated earlier know that love is an experience that began with God. It is agape love, the divine stamina and the heritage of our creation. One week later on or around September 26, 1990, I got a call from my Dean Witter Reynolds broker, Greg Watts. He stated he got a call from Mrs. Emil Parker saying she wanted him to mail her Evelyn's Dean Witter Reynolds IRA account money. Greg Watts told her he could not legally do that. Thus, for the failure of the corrupt Mecklenburg Probate Clerk to do her job and to protect Evelyn; on October 6, 1990, I filed action in Mecklenburg Superior Court. The Judge, Robert Johnston, said I could not represent myself Pro Se in his Court; and that I would have to hire myself a Mecklenburg attorney. Thus, I hired Daniel J. Clifton, and he got Judge Robert Johnston to issue Temporary Restraining Order (TRO) on Thursday October 11, 1990. The TRO Judge Johnston signed, prohibited Evelyn Sanders or any of her agents, and all her agents from pulling out more than $250 from the two retirement Individual Retirement Accounts. That is, they could only pull out $250 from the total of $49,000 that was in the two retirement funds; for which I was the beneficiary and that I owned 50% of the $49,000, approximately $24,500.

However, fear not for here marches in attorney Edward Booker Jr. of Davidson, North Carolina. Edward Booker Jr. is another profligate, impure attorney in North Carolina. For attorney Edward Booker Jr., hired by Mrs. Emil Parker, did not give a royal care about Judge Robert Johnston. Booker knew himself to be above the law. He has been in criminal contempt for over sixteen years of

Judge Johnston's Temporary Restraining Order, (TRO), signed as stated on October 11, 1990. For Edward Booker Jr. also committed criminal Notary Forgery on October 15, 1990. For Edward Booker Jr. notarized with his North Carolina Notary stamp a new forged signature of Evelyn Sanders in a new change of beneficiary on October 15, 1990. Of course, this was four days after Judge Johnston's TRO, signed on October 11, 1990, which is a criminal felony by Edward Booker. Additionally, pursuant to ERISA and REACT signed by U.S. Congress into law, Booker has performed criminal racketeering and committed various criminal felonies. He should have been indicted, prosecuted, and convicted and sent off to prison for several years. However again, Mecklenburg Solicitor, nor any other state official has the guts to do the right thing. However, I, by an affidavit and letter to North Carolina Secretary of State, did manage to get Booker's Notary stamp revoked. If justice is to be rendered by North Carolina, some guilty agents have to be indicted and prosecuted. Subsequently on November 4, 1990, Judge Robert Johnston signed the Preliminary Injunction that said 50% of retirement money was mine, Launeil Sanders. How do you get the officials in authority, power and prestige to do the right thing and hold accountable other government officials, attorneys, officers of the Court? As police officers and infected attorneys who commit criminal misconduct, criminal felonies as officers of the Court, seems to me, to get free passes. They think they are untouchable, and that they can do anything they wish.

So Honorable Judge Robert Johnston, how can you stand for any justice in North Carolina when you let Edward Booker Jr. say to you "I'm above the Law, to hell with your TRO and Preliminary Injunction; I'm a cocky attorney and can commit criminal contempt of your TRO and Preliminary Injunction, and I won't be touched!" America's legal system is corrupted with many, depraved and rotten attorneys. A great deal of these same putrescent attorneys run and are elected to Congress and the U. S. Senate.

At that hearing that was conducted on October 22, 1990, and before Mecklenburg Superior

Court Judge Robert Johnston, my attorney Daniel J. Clifton represented me. The two sisters in law hired attorney Edward Booker Jr. After sworn testimony from me, Judge Robert Johnston ruled that none of Evelyn's agents (including attorney Edward Booker Jr.) could remove only $250 from either the Fidelity or Dean Witter Reynolds retirement accounts. He additionally said I could visit Evelyn on Friday October 26, 1990. Mrs. Emil Parker had prohibited me from seeing or visiting with my own wife since July 10, 1990. I sincerely wish that our Senators and Congressman would pass some federal legislation with stiff penalties for those who perform assisted suicide!

On November 4, 1990, Judge Johnston issued his Preliminary Injunction ruling that only ½ (one-half) of the retirement account money could be pulled out. This resulted in that only approximately $24,500 could be removed. However, as previously stated, the fraudulent, deviate Edward Booker Jr. had already committed criminal notary forgery and criminal contempt of Judge Johnston's TRO signed on October 11, 1990, and the Preliminary Injunction signed on November 4, 1990. Booker committed criminal racketeering and criminal felonies by changing the beneficiaries on October 15, 1990, a criminal change of beneficiary of the Dean Witter Reynolds account on that Monday October 15, 1990, four days after Judge Johnston's October 11, 1990, TRO. However, to this day, no prosecution has been brought against Booker for his criminal racketeering, or against Dean Witter Reynolds for their criminal contempt and racketeering. Thus, they pulled out 100% of the IRA retirement money, and to this date, I have never, ever seen a penny of my entitled ½ of the retirement money. Thus, the premise still holds: "There is no search for truth and justice in Mecklenburg County, State of North Carolina Legal System."

I tried to get relief in the North Carolina justice system. However, I failed. For if you do not punish corrupt attorney officers of the Court for performance and committing of criminal felonies, criminal Notary Forgery, and criminal contempt of Superior Judge Robert Johnston's TRO (October 11, 1990, and Preliminary Injunction November 4, 1990), then the whole justice system fails.

INFINITE STRUGGLE TO REGAIN CUSTODY OF MY TWO CHILDREN AFTER DEATH OF MY SPOUSE EVELYN

After Evelyn died in November 29, 1990, I thought I could regain custody of my two children from the Gaston Court. After she died, the Gaston Court removed Judge Catherine Stevens and replaced her with Judge Timothy Patti. However, I would eventually find out how rigged the whole Gaston legal system was. That Judge Patti always favored in house counsel, attorney James Carpenter and polluted police officer, sister in law Georgia West. All were officers of the Gaston Court, and it was rigged, illegally conspired against me from the very beginning. Judge Timothy Patti willfully recklessly violated the North Carolina Supreme Court precedent setting case law in James v. Pretlow, 242 NC 102, 104 86 S.E.2d 759, 761 (1955); as in the case when one of biological parents died the children were granted to an Aunt. The North Carolina Supreme Court ruled that the surviving spouse has entire sovereignty and supremacy over any and all third parties. Moreover, in other North Carolina Supreme Court cases, state precedent setting case law, the biological parents have extreme absolute sovereignty over other third parties. In another *starre decisis* precedent by North Carolina Appeals Court; Comer v. Comer, 61 N.C. App324, 300 S.E.2d 457 (1983), biological parents rights are protected! It notes that where one parent is deceased, the surviving biological parent has a natural and legal right to custody and control of the minor children. As right now in 2006, my biological daughter, Natalie Caroline Sanders has had at least two criminal abortions; my son lived in fornication, adultery with his girlfriend almost two years before he married her. How can any decent God-Fearing individual concur anything other than when Judge Stevens signed an Emergency Custody Order on that fateful day of July 25, 1990, (case # 90-CVD-2566), she, Stevens, sentenced them to death? North Carolina, through its State Judicial System sentenced them to live, learn and mock the same devilish corrupt lifestyle of the devil for which the Catherine Stevens sentenced them to live in! They were sentenced to live in the household of the devil. This was a household of four fornicators, adulterers: Georgia West fornicating with Jim Anderson, still married to his wife, Judy Anderson; and her oldest son, Issac West Jr., and his live-in fornicator, adulterer, girlfriend and their illegitimate baby born in June 1990, just a month before 90-CVD-2566. Judge Patti didn't care at all about the North Carolina Supreme Court cases noted above. Patti was more interested in ruling for his in-house profligate fat boy counsel Carpenter and contaminated in-house police officer Georgia West. Patti also ruled against me on October 31, 1991, in the Order he issued. That since I was acting Pro Se, Georgia West's little attorney, James Carpenter, drafted the Order that Patti signed. And God for bid, guess who had to pay this fornicator, adulterer's legal fees? Well, I had to pay this crooked, bent James Carpenter the $2500.00 legal fees, or I would have had to serve 30 days in jail. If you were really naïve about America's Legal system and the Gaston family law District Court system as I was at this time, you had to endure all these fornicators, adulterers! I do not know if any of you remember one of the Miller Lite ™ beer commercials several years ago. This commercial showed a husband who had just gotten a divorce. In this commercial, the lawyer, (the scum sucking bottom feeding scavenger) had been lassoed and taken down. The lawyer literally took everything he owned. I do believe some of the marketing or advertising employees on Wall Street who had been recently involved in Family Court of America and the shenanigans of these putrid deviate attorneys prepared this commercial. Later, the American Bar Association demanded this advertisement be stopped, and Miller caved in! For most of America consists of triple corrupt attorneys, with a whole bunch in Washington, and it is affecting America. They did not have a right to steal my two biological children; and then, deny me rights of visitation with them!

Everyone should read Alec Baldwin's book "about divorce and child custody" when it is published as Mr. Baldwin has also been standing in the gap for Jesus and fighting! In 1991 I knew that the law of precedent cases such as James v. Pretlow, 242 N.C. 102, 104 86 S.E.2d 759, 761 (1955); and Comer v. Comer, 61 N.C. App 324, 300 S.E.2d 457 (1983) were on my side. However, the premise still holds as when you go up against tainted officers of the Court and a sister in law, Georgia West, who is a putrid, depraved Gastonia cop and officer of the Court, James Carpenter, crooked fat boy counsel, you cannot lose! It has already predetermined that you cannot win. It is rigged against you. That is the real definition of bias, prejudice, and partiality in America's courts. You do not have a chance, even if you have 1000 attorneys representing you! Judy Anderson knew how triple corrupt the Gaston legal system was, and that why she told me "her husband Jim Anderson and Georgia West deserved each other." You see I really know why divorce and child custody attorneys and judges are being killed in America. As just this week, June 20, 2006, this Reno, Nevada, pawnshop proprietor, Darren Roy Mack, killed his wife, Charla Mack, and shot Nevada family law court Judge Chuck Weller, who did not die from his wounds. There are many, many more family cases in America where deadly violence has entered into the picture. If our Congressmen/women and Senators don't sign into law a New Federal Divorce and Child Custody Law that spells out more Godly details, things will get worse. One of the mandatory provisions in this new bill should be that child visitation is mandatory to be given to both parents unless one is in a prison institution. The provisions of this new bill would be enforceable by U.S. Federal Marshals. If this does not happen, more murders and killings will occur.

26

There is no justice in all of the family law courts in all our fifty states of this nation. It is just like the large family of India and Pakistan. When they split away in 1948 into the two countries, the grudges, the hatred, hateful evil spirits of the devil have devoured the people in trying to get even. It is just the same as what is happening in our nation's family law courts. As mentioned, the Custody Order issued by Judge Timothy Patti in Gaston District Court on October 31, 1991, in 90-CVD-2566 was illegal. I anticipated severe problems, but just did not think they could steal my own biological children.

Judge Timothy Patti's Order on October 31, 1991, in 90-CVD-2566 stated that I had to pay Carpenter's $2500.00 fees {Georgia West's counsel and her attorney fees}; or if I refused, I would have to serve 30 days in Gaston jail for contempt. Well, of course, you are aware that James Carpenter drafted the Order for Judge Patti. That's standard practice in all the courts of our land. Judges are lazy, casual and extremely pompous. Since most judges were once attorneys who had to draft judges' orders, now they have graduated into being able to utilize this fringe extreme benefit of being a judge. The good old boys and good old girls rule in triple infected Gaston County. I am not the first in our country to be victimized by the corrupt family law systems for our great country. That is why I hope to give testimony to Congress on why a New Federal National Enhancement Family Law Bill is required. That will do away with these triple injustices in America, which had been alluded to earlier. Our forefathers envisioned a different America. Thus, I propose the following new federal legislation: Proposed New Federal Family Law for Divorce and Child Custody. This would, I pray, that our Congress would pass sometime in the future: That the ***New Federal Law for Divorce and Child Custody*** will be standardized with exact forms that would be filed in U.S. Federal District Courts.

1. (A man, male, and a wife, female; Married in Holy Matrimony as husband and wife) may file these forms in any U S Federal District Court. No lawyer fees would be charged in family disputes. However, both parties would have to mandatory attend and complete "Negotiation, Mediation Training", and that this completed training would have to be submitted to the U.S. Federal District

Judge for a final Divorce and /or Child Custody Resolution Order to be issued. No lawyer fees could be assessed to either parent, nor would lawyers be required or allowed to achieve this function in U.S. Federal Court.

2. That "Joint Custody is Mandatory", and in only where one parent is in prison serving life sentence or on death row for a criminal felony could one parent win sole custody. That is, if one parent lived in California, and other parent lived in North Carolina, the worst visitation one of parents could receive would be the visitation during the three, (3), summer months of school vacation of any minor children who were attending school. That this child visitation would be federally enforceable through the U.S. Federal Marshals nation-wide across the 50 states! One of pit-falls of current state laws now is that one parent shuns or just disregards orders from other states. There is no justice from previous state family law cases. As just like in my case, you have a putrid, defiled sister in law who is a member, officer of the Court, of Gaston County, North Carolina, that never, ever had legal jurisdiction. Georgia West knew well how the corrupt Gaston family law system worked and knew she could whip me in her favorable court. She could sue Evelyn and me in Gaston District Court, and simply steal my two biological children. Why did the family law judge in Hilton Head Island, South Carolina, rule against the biological mother because she was a wealthy real-estate agent making over six, (6), figure salary. She was not entitled to custody; but the judge awarded full custody to the father who was less wealthy? Well, because the Judge is just another, bias, prejudiced, pompous, close knit family law judge that adheres to the basic premise: "If you have the most polluted attorney who knows the most contaminated judge that can be distorted, and manipulated, then you cannot lose." Why did the man in Clayton, Missouri, go into the family law court and kill his wife, her attorney, and the family law judge? Again, the same basic premise is that family law court has nothing to do about "truth and justice." Justice cannot be found in America's family law courts. The basic premise is as follows: If you have the most deviate attorney who knows the most defiled judge that can be distorted and

contaminated, then you cannot lose. There was another case with a Michigan couple involved in a custody battle. CBS "48 Hours" profiled this case as a mother was claiming that the father had sexually abused the children. The father spent $85,000 of attorney and legal fees to prove her charges were false. The Michigan family law judge ruled and awarded custody back to the father. This case shows why Congress should sign a new federal law making it mandatory of joint custody of the children and prohibit any more criminal dirty tricks by lawyers.

There are many, many more cases in our state law systems where state precedent laws have been violated. Our children are on loan to us from God. We, as their parents, are to strive to raise them as God commanded us! Nevertheless, in America today, just like our government, we hold no party accountable! Well, we all are sinners. We will be held accountable to God for our disobedience to God. I commend the U.S. Supreme Court for agreeing to hear a present case before them. Why did the child support attorney in Orange, California, get murdered by one of parents who had just lost custody of his children? Again, these parents, just as I, understand it is not fair, but entirely corrupt.

Those of us who will resort to violence immediately, will act like the man in Clayton, Missouri. He was asked why he did it. He stated, "The Judge had taken God's gifts and had taken everything I had worked for my entire life." Thus, Congress must pass new legislation in order to stop the killings. Well, back to the time line as Judge Timothy Patti, on October 31, 1991, gave full custody of my two biological children to the one and only fornicator, adulterer Georgia West. I had been trying to track down Georgia West's adopted daughter Janice West. On November 3, 1991, I found out she was living with her sister in Lincolnton, North Carolina. I went to see her on November 6, 1991. I knew that Georgia West had had her committed to Broughton Hospital Institution several times. I wanted to see how she could help me get my children back from her stepmother. Janice West was living in a mobile home trailer with no heat, no bathroom, no refrigerator or stove and had a mattress on floor in one of rooms to sleep on. She had to go over to her sister's house to eat and use restroom. I told her I had three bedrooms in my house in Spartanburg, and if she wanted to come down and live with me, I would rent her one of the bedrooms. That we could draw up a rental agreement. She accepted. That Friday evening we drove back to Spartanburg, South Carolina. I knew Georgia West would be thoroughly upset. However, why would Georgia West let her live in the conditions I found her, if there was any love for her? In Court when Georgia West was asked the whereabouts of Janice West, her adopted daughter, she lied. I drew up the rental agreement for $200.00 per month. Janice told me Georgia West never treated her right. She always treated her worst than she treated her two biological sons, Issac and Benjamin.

Thus, I was so upset that this Judge Patti had given Georgia West custody of my biological children, that I decided that Janice West and I would sue the North Carolina Judicial Standards Commission. I paid the $55.00 and Janice West and I filed it in Gaston District Court on November 18, 1991. I knew Chip Wilson over at the Gaston Observer newspaper and he printed it in the paper. By gosh, if you do not think this really got their attention, you would be wrong. However, it brought the whole system with more force on me. I had a hearing on our lawsuit on January 6, 1992. Since my $ 931.00 December 31, 1991, child support was five days late, Patti issued an arrest warrant. After our hearing, I was arrested. I spent eight hours in the Gaston jail until a friend of mine in Charlotte, North Carolina, Mr. Dwight Wessler, came down and paid my $931.00. I immediately reimbursed Dwight in his car that afternoon. I wrote him a check for $931.00. Of course, the Gaston Court would not take a personal check, and they knew that I probably did not have $931.00 cash on me. I really did appreciate Dwight's help; thanks again Dwight for being a genuine God-fearing friend. Again, I know God is always in control! I am writing this as the way I felt at that time, and if I were a violent person I would have tried to kidnap my children back. However, I knew if God wanted me to endure these trials, I was going to be up to the challenge. I knew Georgia West had tremendous power and authority. She was with Jim Anderson and others. In 2007 now, I have heard that Georgia West Anderson is no longer a police officer.

Janice West and I went to six different attorneys, and no one wanted to take on the North Carolina Judicial Standards Commission. Thus, Janice and I filed a voluntary dismissal. Nevertheless, one thing came out of the suit later that year. Chief Postell of the City of Gastonia Police Department said to Georgia West and Jim Anderson that they would have to quit shacking up and fornicating with each other. I believe, "according to Janice West", Georgia and Jim Anderson got married in November 1992. When I started my new job in Tampa, Florida, I helped Janice get her a mobile home in Spartanburg, South Carolina.

5

MY NEW JOB WITH RAYTHEON ENGINEERS AND CONSTRUCTORS IN TAMPA, FLORIDA

That I believe it did help me to take the job in Tampa, and it had only been six months since I received

my pink slip layoff from Fluor Daniel in Greenville. I was required to perform considerable amount of

travel on this new job, and I was excited about getting some Christian pen pals in the Philippines. I

had joined a Christian Club and set a goal of possibly marrying a Philippine Christian Lady. I wanted

God to grant us some more children, if God could find that right Christian woman for me. I knew that

the Philippine people were devout, pious, earnest and solemn family orientated. That I wanted family

devout people such as was of our forefathers who originally established our country. (faith in God,

country and family) I am an optimist, and even though all these things had happened to me, I never

gave up my faith in God and Jesus Christ. I had not blamed God for my trials and tribulations. I kept

my faith in that perseverance in that God would lead me in the righteous path. At this time of my life,

I was still putting my faith somewhat in man's law. I thought I would not keep losing all the legal

battles in Court. However, I was wrong. Until I learned to do it God's way, God would know I was not ready!

The first letter I received back from the Philippines was from a nurse (Evelyn had been a nurse), and her name was Kathryn Eschevez. I believe she was 26 years old. She wrote me a very nice, pleasant letter. She had a Philippine boy friend, and they were planning to get married in two to three years. Since I told her my wife had died of liver cancer in 1990; she noticed that she thought I was in a mighty hurry to get married. Truth is that I was. I was married to Evelyn for fifteen years, and these three years of single life were miserable. I wrote to several other girls and received several responses. I continued to respond to these ladies, and I continued to get excited about marrying myself a Christian lady from a foreign country. And on January 24, 1993, I received the first letter from a Christian lady named Janneth Aguinaldo Emberador. She sent me two pictures, and I have one of those pictures today. The other picture was used to apply for a visa for Janneth. For it was what she said in the first letter that I knew God had guided a true Christian lady into my life. I felt God would really be disappointed in me if I did not present myself honorably and decently in order to try and persuade her to marry me. Thus, I pressed on with God's guidance. You know, I did not think I deserved to have my two biological children kidnapped and stolen by Georgia West. I knew she had driven the spikes in me, and knew she was an exploiting, profiteering, fraudulent police officer. However, if it was God's will, I was going to marry a Christian Philippine lady whom God had brought into my life half way around the world. And if God blessed our Holy marriage with children, we would be a Godly family.

Shown on the neighboring pages are the following photos: <u>photograph 4, Janneth in her blue dress; graphic 5, Janneth's Love is Priceless letter mailed to me from her in Philippines; and photograph 52, which is the first photo that Janneth sent me in January 1993 in her yellow dress and hat outfit.</u> I am lucky {blessed by the grace of God!} that this lady is my wife now. God blessed us with a daughter Dorothy Love Sanders, born in December 1994. And Colonel Launeil Tony Sanders

33

was born on June 2003. I truly know God had a purpose in all my trials and tribulations; however it was difficult in those 1990, 1991, 1992 and 1993 years. And February 3, 1994, when Janneth arrived at the Tampa airport, I initiated a new beginning. I listen to Pastor Greg Laurie who is pastor of Harvest Crusades of Riverside, California. Both our vehicles are tuned to Blue Ridge Broadcasting, 106.9 FM out of Black Mountain, North Carolina. They have Christian programming such as Greg Laurie's Harvest Crusades and others. I know God had Janneth praying for me long before I ever met her. Most people think you can get a visa approved immediately. It doesn't work that way with America's immigration agency. I first went to visit and meet Janneth in April 1993, but it took us eleven months to get her visa approved and for her to arrive in Tampa.

One of the first assignments at Raytheon was in La Plata, Argentina, South America, for a one and half million dollars environmental World Bank feasibility study. I was assigned to the World Bank project. I was responsible for the gaseous effluents and the hazardous solid waste effluents. I had Mike Cohen to assist me; and we had approximately 66% of the project. We traveled to Buenos Aires, Argentina, September 22, 1992. We were in Argentina for six weeks, and I made a real friend in Mike Cohen. Mike had a wife and two children. His oldest son was attending the University of Florida in Gainesville. We went out to dinner together and spent a great deal of time together. One of the things I remember Mike saying, "Well Neil, are we having fun, and do we have the Big Picture?" Mike did not have a real strong environmental background; however he possessed excellent computer strengths. I was curious what Mike might be doing today.

All of the restaurants in Argentina were excellent. The beef was great. Mike and I enjoyed the Expo World 1992, which was held in Buenos Aires on Columbus Day. Some of the Argentine models that were there were very beautiful. There were some very pretty Argentine foreign women, and it energized me more since I was planning to marry a Christian Philippine lady. After we got back to the

United States in November 1, 1992, Mike and I compiled our report. It had been over two years since Evelyn died. And the corrupt Gaston Court would not let me see my children; however each month I sent my $931.00 to the Gaston Court clerk to give to Georgia West. Really, God let's you make choices in this earthly world. I knew that it wasn't fair. But I am an optimist, and put my enthusiasm and energy in trying to marry a Christian Philippine lady as God wanted me to do.

I didn't hire a full time nurse for Evelyn, and that was a mistake. I did not have any domestic conflicts. I never hit my wife or my two children, and don't have any police reports against me. I guess I really didn't know how lost I was. I thought you could always do it yourself. I thought you could do it with man's expertise. But the only way to eternity is to publicly accept Jesus Christ as your personal savior, repent and turn from your sins, and begin anew. You must have your faith in Christ and let Christ walk with you in all the trials and tribulations of life in this earthly world.

So I was angry and really didn't fully understand God's plan for my life. In the Bible there's "What goes around Comes Around!" Revenge is with the Lord. Even though I had this corrupt sister in law who kidnapped my two biological children, I did not fully understand that God had me traveling through the trials and tribulations of His Plan. God needed to fully prepare me just as he did for Moses. I know that God was and is always in Control. And I didn't enjoy this trial and tribulation that God had planned for me.

One of the second assignments at Raytheon was in Curacao, West Indes, at the Curacao refinery in the Caribbean. On this project I was the lead on gathering, sampling and performing drilling samples on the Curacao Refinery. Our main objectives were to determine the extent of soil contamination, underground wells contamination and underground water pollution. My first trip was in December 1992. This occurred from December 14, 1992 until December 22, 1992. This involved a preliminary survey and determination of total number of wells, soil samples and hazardous wastes

July 7, 1993

To (my) dear (sweet laurin)
Have a nice day! I hope this is
surprising upon finding this letter of mine
with all my heart its so great exciting when
you are by my side forever.

You know theres nothing more priceless
less than love, Im truely love you deep in
my heart. My lovers embrace my treasure
that within no measure, in the sight of god Im
also know that I have never loved anyone as
much as I love you. God surely gifted to my
heart you that I love you.
I believed that laurinel was
word to love me til the day of her life, I
love everything you said at your care,
that you send it to me.

MILLION of thanks that you love
for me very truly.

Remember these words; you are the
most important part of my life next to god
I do need you very much. Im your
with you, you are my everything and that love
to me.

your future wife,

LOVE & care; JANNETH.....

*There's nothing
more priceless
than love...
and thanks to you
I feel like I'm one of
the richest people
in the world,
because with you I have
all the love
I'll ever need."*

sweetheart laurin)
do to your care that you keep
it to me family it a weeping the union
of two hearts, keeping one promise one
life _____ forever one

may god watch over you
it will always
love
you.

a ___ A love
is a simple of love

may god bless you always;

as laurinel realizing that she loves laurinel
moreover of its mother, father & sisters
coz she believed of its family. day hello
to your children and your mom & dad, I love
you all as I love you very much.
sincerely your caring wife,
Love & care; Janneth

TO MY MOST PRECIOUS THING (SWEET JANNETH) HELLO! HAVE A GREAT DAY! THY WORDS OF THE LORD SHALL KEEP YOUR HEART & MIND THAT ANY GOD GRANT YOU STRENGTH AND PEACE.. REMEMBER! YOU KNOW YOU'RE THE ONE I SAVED MYSELF TO TAKE COUR- AGED TO LIVE IN THIS EARTHLY WORLD. I'M ALWAYS THINK INTO THE LORD FOR GIVING ME A SPECIAL SOMEONE THAT GOD GRANTED ME, FOR YOU. I CAN DO EVERYTHING TO MAKE YOU HAPPY ON THAT MOMENT. I DO SO MUCH PRAYING AND BELIEVED OF OUR LORD JESUS CHRIST OUR SAVIOR EVERY- THING'S FINE FOR YOU AND FOR ME. I TELL YOU THERE SWEET, BE ON GUARD LOYALLY PRECIOUS BODDY COZ YOUR HONEY BABY JANNETH IT'S SO VERY FAR AWAY FOR YOU.

I LOVE YOU NEVER ENDING. I TELLING YOU THERE BECAUSE I'M A LUCKY GIRL, I MADE MYLIFE A SPECIAL SOMEONE, I KNOW YOU ARE SAVED IF YOU WILL LEAVE IN THIS EARTHLY WORLD. AND I KNOW YOU ARE IN HEAVEN. AND I'M ALSO SAME...

YOURS ?

THE BIBLE PROMISES, BELIEVE IN THE LORD JESUS AND YOU WILL BE SAVED.

SWEET;

"I'm sure it takes a lot of courage and determination to do what you're doing. I just wanted to let you know how much I admire and care about you and how often I'll be praying that God will strengthen you and grant you His wonderful peace."

"GOD LOVE US," THE BIBLE SAYS! LET ALL YOUR THINGS BE DONE WITH LOVE.

"I HOPE YOU WILL BE HAPPY OH ALWAYS! SWEET DREAM AND A MILLION OF HUGS AND KISSES.

PRAYING FOR YOU ALWAYS, LOVE & CARE; JANNETH

drum samples to be collected. The next trip was scheduled in January 25, 1993 to February 20, 1993. On January 24, 1993, (the day before we departed for Curacao) I received my first letter from Janneth Emberador. After reading her letter and discovering that she was a Bible Baptist Christian, I was extremely excited. I decided to take my Raytheon vacation last week of April and first week of May 1993 to go to the Philippines. After the Curacao trip, I mailed Janneth some pictures. What most Americans don't probably know is that there are a lot of restrictions; and it is not easy to obtain a visa for someone in a foreign country. If we were to be married in America, Janneth and I would have to be in the marriage for three years before she would be eligible for Naturalization as a U.S. Naturalized Citizen. The visa forms and accompanying guidelines said you had to include a $75.00 application fee and that it would take 60 days. These sixty days written estimate were totally inaccurate, as it took eleven months for me to obtain her visa approval. Our U.S. government cannot do anything fast.

On the preceding is photograph 6, formal tux photos I sent Janneth. Therefore, in March 1993 I paid the $75.00 immigration fees and mailed all materials to the U.S. Immigration and Naturalization Office. And I made my plane reservations to go to Philippines in last week of April 26, 1993, through May 10, 1993. I put in for my vacation time. When Mike Cohen and I went to lunch daily, I shared with him a picture of Janneth. I promised myself that when I arrived, met Janneth and all her family, that I would not have any sexual relations. I wanted her to marry me and be my eternity partner here in the rest of my time in this earthly world. And in my two weeks there, we did not have sexual relations; we were abstinent. I thought maybe the visa would be approved, and she could fly back with me. However, I was to later learn that was not going to happen. But this two weeks' trip to meet Janneth was the best trip of my life. She knew that my spouse of fifteen years had died of liver cancer, and I was truthful to her. I also told her my two children lived up in North Carolina with a sister in law. However, I did not volunteer all information on my legal battles with Georgia West, as I was scared she might not marry me if I mentioned all these complications. I told her my children would not be living with us in my house in Spartanburg, South Carolina. I thoroughly enjoyed my fellowship with Janneth and her family. In one of letters from Janneth before I went to see her, Janneth said she would like to have one or two children; and that she thought she would be a good mother! This really excited me as I told her I wanted some more children, and I really knew that Jesus Christ was working in my life! While I was in the Philippines during the two weeks visit, I went to U.S. Immigration Office in Manila twice.

And toward the last four days of my trip, I realized that Janneth would not be coming back with me. I was really depressed, and would be more depressed after I arrived back to Tampa, Florida, and found the letter from U.S. Immigration and Naturalization Service, denying my petition. They had denied my petition. The law required that we were to have met personally in the past two years. Now, that I had just come back from meeting her; I had met that requirement of the law. The materials said that I could file an appeal to U.S. INS, and that I would have to file an additional $110.00 appeal fee along with appeal to U.S. Immigration and Naturalization Agency. I immediately filed the appeal with my fees along with my plane receipts and my credit cards receipts in Cebu, Philippines. Every time you file papers with the U.S. Immigration and Naturalization you have to include more money. Additionally I wrote my first letter to Honorable U.S. Senator Bob Graham from Florida requesting his assistance in getting Janneth's visa approved. In July 15, 1993, I got a pink slip from Raytheon; this was a reduction in work force and the work force reduction slip didn't come from my boss, Jeffrey Bryant. Bryant was the head of the Environmental Department. Bryant was in Brazil on a business development trip trying to get jobs from the Brazil steel industries. Of the 160 employees at the Tampa, most were in Process Engineering Department. This department had all the clout with the managers. And in March the United Engineers & Constructors in Philadelphia had won the power struggle with the Raytheon's Boston office. Since United Engineers & Constructors Inc. had won the power battle, the engineers in Boston were laid off, and the Tampa office also had lay offs. The United Engineers people in Philadelphia would be calling all the shots. I sent out a lot of resumes in Tampa, Florida, area. I believed that because of my age and the higher salary, I was having great difficulty in obtaining new employment. I was being discriminated against because of my age. It is just a fact of life in America when you get older. Our government is not enforcing the current Age Discrimination in Employment Act (ADEA) passed by Congress.

Thus, I signed up for my unemployment; however I only could draw benefits for six months. In the meantime I kept sending out resumes. I received notice from the U.S. Immigration and Naturalization Service that on July 20, 1993, that Janneth's visa had been approved. So now, I was really excited. I thought Janneth would be to America soon. But I was soon to find out again that our government couldn't do anything in a reasonable timely manner. I had to send an "affidavit of support" to Immigration and Naturalization Service in Manila, Philippines, swearing that I would provide all of Janneth's support, and that America's taxpayers would not pay any money for her ninety days visa. I filed the affidavit. Finally, in November 1, 1993, I wrote my second letter to U.S. Senator Bob Graham and asked him a second time to help me in Janneth's visa. As her visa was approved on July 20, 1993; and I didn't understand why the U. S. Immigration and Naturalization Service was holding up the processing of her visa to America.

And in December 15, 1993, I wrote my third letter to U.S. Senator Bob Graham, just before I went to Memphis to spend Christmas and New Year's with Mother and Harold. The same day I got a wire from Janneth that the U. S. Immigration and Naturalization Service had scheduled to start her processing of her visa in January 2, 1994. And that she needed $500.00 U.S. dollars to cover the Philippines passport, medical exams, transportation and other fees. On December 16, 1993, I wired her the money and went to Memphis for the holidays with Mother and Harold. I had not had a job for past five months, and now my unemployment was exhausted. However, I was still extremely excited because I knew after the first of year Janneth Aguinaldo Emberador was coming to America. Boy was I happy! It seemed like I was going to get to marry Janneth, and if it were God's will he would bless up with a baby!

After the holidays I returned to Tampa. On February 2, 1994, I received notice from U.S. Immigration and Naturalization Service and Philippine Airlines that she would be arriving in Tampa, Florida, on February 3, 1994. That morning when Janneth arrived at the Tampa airport it was the coldest day of the year at 34 degrees Fahrenheit; however it was the warmest day in my heart in over four years. I was excited! I was in love with Janneth, and if it were God's will we would be married in America. When she arrived that morning she was tired. She had flown almost 19 hours including the five hours red eye flight from Los Angeles. She had cleared U.S. Customs at Los Angeles International Airport. Janneth had her baptism in 1987 in Free Will Bible Baptist Church in the Cebu, Philippines. I would like to thank all the churches and missionaries of America who send their members out on mission trips to save lost souls as Jesus taught us he wanted done! For here I am now benefiting from God's work and all the God-fearing work of the missionaries in the Philippines! Maybe, if it is God's will Janneth, Dot Love, Colonel Sanders and I will become missionaries and go back to Philippines to share the "Good News of Jesus Christ" and witness for Christ.

Janneth has told me many times as there is 93% Catholic and abut 7% Protestant in the country of the Philippines. Janneth, her two sisters and her Mother, Juanita Emberador, and her Father, Antonio Emberador were baptized in the Baptist ministry by the Free Will Baptist ministry organized by the Free Will Baptist Church of Independence, Missouri. Janneth told me that they were poked fun towards them by many unbelievers in Cebu, Philippines, after their baptism for taking their Bibles to

church down the streets of Cebu. Janneth and her family were developing their daily devotional and daily personal relationship with Jesus Christ, theirs and our personal savior. That February 3, 1994, Janneth arrived in America. As I told you, Janneth was a virgin and had not had relations with a man in her life. We called Mother and Harold the next morning, and asked them again if it were all right for us to get married in their church, Cumberland Presbyterian Church, Atoka, Tennessee, on Saturday February 26, 1994. They said yes.

LAUNEIL SANDERS MARRIES JANNETH AGUINALDO EMBERADOR

Realization was that Janneth was now in Tampa. After some twelve months when I first applied for her visa she was finally in America to Tampa. In a few days we traveled back to Spartanburg, South Carolina. That we would soon travel to Memphis to get married was so exhilarating. I knew God had delivered the Christian lady he wanted me to share my life with. I was not going to be so lonely any more, as now I was going to have a lifetime partner. I knew that I was strong willed, and that my perseverance would eventually pay-off. The Bible tells us all that. It had now been 3 ½ years since Evelyn died, and because of this fornicator, adulterer Georgia West, I had not been allowed to see my two children for almost four years since July 23, 1990, after Georgia West kidnapped them. I couldn't see my two biological children, but I still have to keep paying this Georgia West $931.00 per month. God is in control! And you can see, when the legal system is rampant with corrupt, evil agents of Satan; and when these evil agents of the Court are in the Gaston County, North Carolina, and you and your family lived in Lincoln County, North Carolina, in the city of Lincolnton, North Carolina and they willfully violate the law, it is rigged corruptly against you.

In the preceding pages shown are the following photographs: photograph 7, husband, Launeil Sanders, and wife, Janneth Sanders, in wedding toast; photograph 8, Launeil Sanders and Janneth Emberador Sanders, husband and wife down the aisle after pronounced Husband and Wife in God's Holy Matrimony Ceremony of God's Marriage; photograph 9, Launeil Sanders and Janneth Emberador Sanders, husband and wife cutting the cake; photograph 10, Launeil Sanders feeding Janneth Emberador Sanders a piece of the cake; photograph 11, group wedding photo of Janneth and Launeil with my sister, Janice Harden to right of Janneth and best man, my brother, George Larry Sanders, to left of me; photograph 12, Launeil Sanders and Janneth Emberador Sanders, with full view of our cake baked by the God- Fearing American Ann Harber; photograph 13, Friends of Launeil and Janneth at reception including top photo, Floyd Craig back to camera, from left of Floyd, Pastor Tracy, Margaret Craig, Ed Cartwright and Betty Cartwright, Harold Craig, Ann Harber, Floyd's daughter and Floyd's wife. Bottom photo, Mickey Criag and sister 's husband Troy Harden and at second table above brother, Larry Sanders, and my aunt, Joan Sanders; photograph 14, group wedding photo of Janneth and Launeil, from the left, step father, Harold Craig, my Mother, Dorothy Craig, my sister, Janice Harden, Janneth, Launeil and my best man, my brother, George Larry Sanders, to left of me.

Janneth and I went to a wedding shop in Tampa to get some wedding invitations the next day. We went to lunch at the Columbian Restaurant. The second day we went to Busch Gardens. The third day we went to Tampa Stadium. The first Sunday we went to Hillandale Baptist Church; and I remember in Sunday school of introducing Janneth. I stated that she had only been in America a few days. I commented in the facts that I had a corrupt sister in law who was a police officer, and that God's saying "what goes around, comes around" does not apply to all people. Someone responded by referring me to Psalm 72.

We sent out the invitations mostly to my relatives in the Memphis area, as none of Janneth's family would be able to attend. If I had known it was going to take one year to get her to America, we could have been married in Cebu, Philippines. But I thought the government's sixty days was realistic! We sent my two children Aaron and Natalie in Cherryville, North Carolina, wedding invitations. But they elected not to come. They had been taught much hatred by this fornicator, adulterer, whom they live with. There needed to be extreme amounts of healing and absorption of Jesus Christ in their hearts to heal all the hatred. We got back to Spartanburg, South Carolina, and went over to Mother and Harold's a week early to take care of matters, including getting our marriage license at Tipton County Court house in Covington, Tennessee. Our Wedding Day: February 26, 1994:

That I truly felt the Lord was going to bless Janneth's and my union, as in our wedding vows Janneth said "By the Grace of God I accept Launeil as my Wedded Husband!" This was a very, very special day in my life. Age did not matter; what really mattered is that God brought me a true Christian lady for whom he wanted me to share the rest of my earthly life! I wanted so much for God to bless us as a family and give us a child! My Mother and step-dad went to Country music on Saturday nights, and they had a circle of friends in this country music. Two were Ed and Betty Cartwright, who were devout Christians. They came to our wedding. Mrs. Ann Harber, who is a God-fearing

American living in that All American city of Millington, Tennessee, baked our wedding cake for our wedding. My cousin, Sandy Sanders, photographed our wedding. "Janneth and I want to sincerely thank Sandy again for his photographs and Ann Harber for our wedding cake of that divine day God granted us." Janneth and I went to country music at International Harvester on our wedding

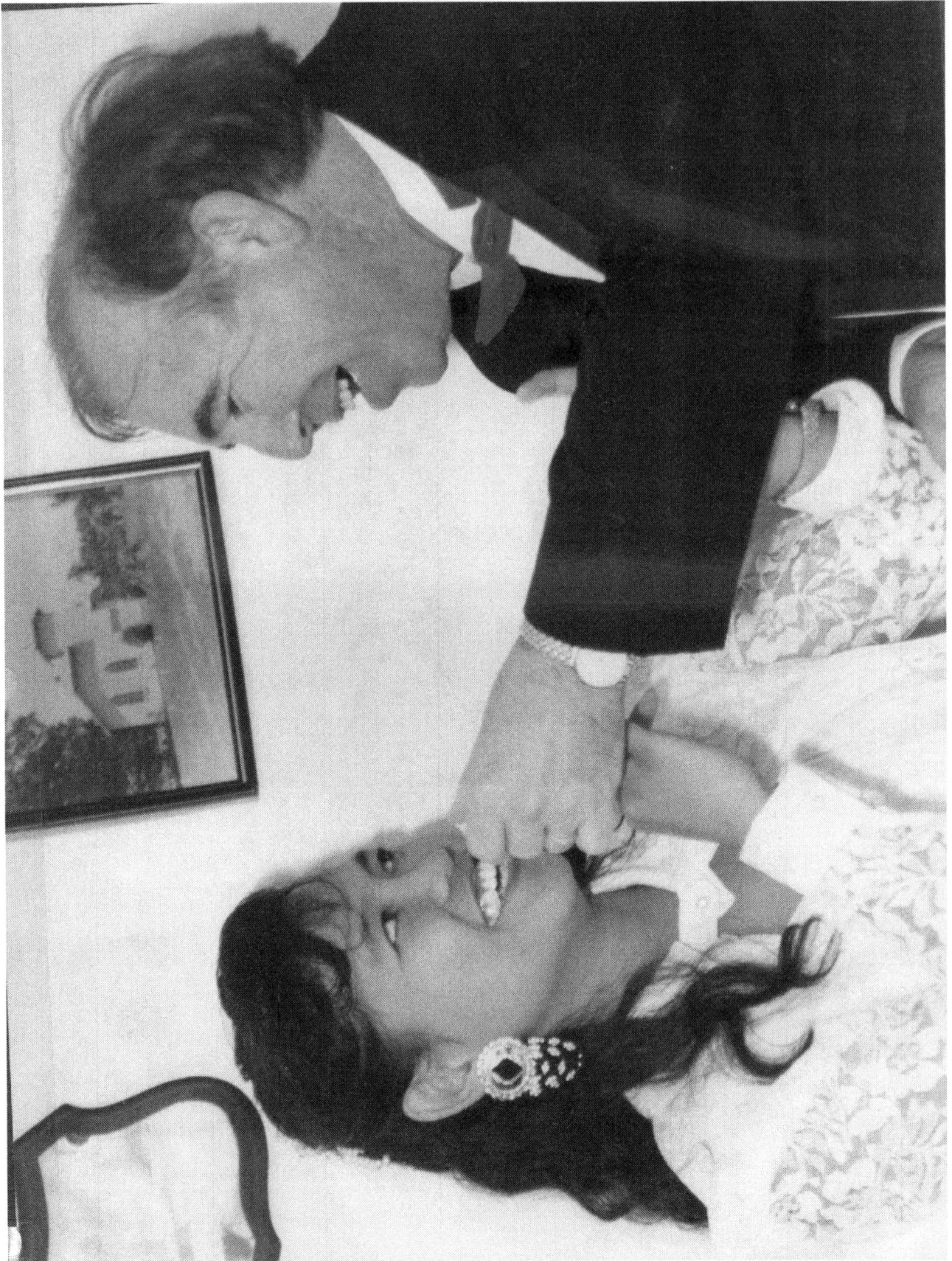

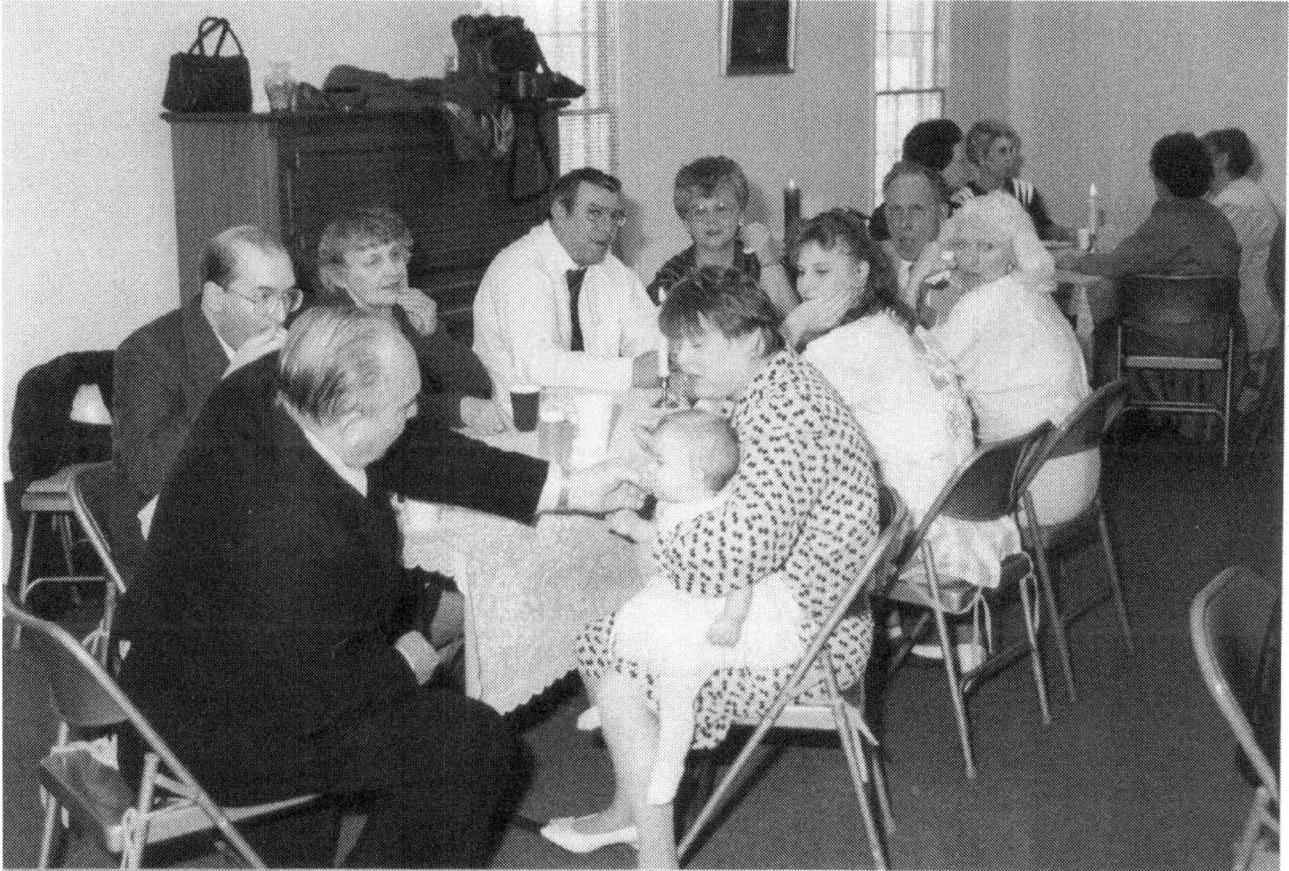

night to hear Ed and Betty Cartwright. I had us reservations at the Residence Inn in Germantown, Tennessee, on our wedding night, that Saturday, February 26, 1994.

I told Harold and Mother when we left the country music Saturday night that we would be back at the house to go to church with them the next morning. I don't believe Harold thought we were serious. You see, the Reverend Randy Tracy, who was Mother and Harold's minister, married us that Saturday, February 26, 1994. Janneth and I consummated our marriage in the house of the Lord earlier that day; and at the Residence Inn consummated "our agape" God's love he granted us on our wedding night. We made it back to Mother and Harold's on Sunday morning to go to church with them. Thus, Reverend Randy Tracy married us in the Holy Matrimony in the house of the Lord. We heard Reverend Tracy on Sunday deliver the message and "the Good News of Jesus Christ" the day after on the Sabbath. Here, now God had blessed my life.

On the preceding pages are several photos: photograph 15, which has two photos with first top of Launeil and Janneth on skiis during one of our honeymoon trips to Telluride ski resort at Telluride, Colorado, and the bottom photo of one of us on our bikes at our home in Spartanburg. The second photo, photograph 16, consists of three skiing photos of Janneth on our honeymoon in Telluride resort. I wanted to go to church with Mother and Harold the day after God had united us. I knew in time now my life was and had already been blessed by God!

Our Two Honeymoons:

I told Mother and Harold that we were going to Orlando, Florida, for a week and go to Disney World and Sea World. I told Mother we would be back, and then we were going to Telluride, Colorado, for a week of snow skiing. At Disney World and Sea World, Janneth and I really had much pleasure, voluptuousness, and satisfaction in the Lord's fellowship. I had us lodging reservations at the Marriott Orlando World, and we ate at the Japanese restaurant, went to several other restaurants and enjoyed ordering, "The special chocolate covered strawberries." The Marriott Orlando World had basketball units in the complex, and Janneth and I really were pleased as Janneth played basketball for their community team. I was really joyous, ecstatic, prosperous and blithesome. I felt that if God would bless us with a child, we would be a devoted God fearing family. As I knew from one of Janneth's letters, she wanted a child. Mother didn't want us to have a baby right away; however I knew if it were God's will, God would bless us. So I didn't talk about having a baby around Mother, even though Janneth and I wished that blessing. Pastor Tracy, when he married us, told us "to go have ten babies." I will always cherish the wedding card Janneth's Mom and father sent us as her Mother, Juanita Emberador, said for "Janneth and Launeil to go procreate a baby." That was exactly the way I felt. I have thanked God for answering my prayers. And at the Marriott Orlando World, we followed Janneth's Mom's instructions.

At the end of the week in Orlando, we drove back to Memphis. We spent one night with Mother and Harold before driving out to Telluride. Of course, Janneth having been raised in the Philippines, had never seen snow in her life. We stayed one Saturday night with Mother and step father Harold and drove the two days to Telluride, Colorado. I had package reservations, which included the five nights of lodging and four days of ski-lift tickets. I knew how to ski as I had taken a lesson at Squaw Valley in December 1984. I knew Janneth would need to enroll in a lesson; and we scheduled it on the first day there.

At Telluride they did not teach the students how to get on and off of the ski lifts; in Squaw Valley this was part of the lesson. And as all skiers know, you don't sit down and stand up in the lift. One has to ski on and ski off the lifts. She did not know how to ski on and off the ski lifts. Thus, Janneth managed to get up and fall a couple of times, before she learned that technique. It snowed every night we were in Telluride. We had great time skiing in the daytime, and enjoying our Honeymoon in the evenings. I was grateful to God for His plan for my life. Praise God for bringing this Christian lady into my life and for granting me the privilege of marrying her. Janneth does not eat beef; it is that in the Philippines she and her Mother never ate beef. It has nothing to do with her religion, as I mentioned earlier, that she is a Christian and was baptized in 1987. She mostly ate pork, chicken and fish with rice at every meal. Thus, since our marriage, I have eaten more chicken, pork, and fish. After our Telluride trip, we returned to Memphis to spend a couple of days with Mother and Harold. We returned home to Spartanburg, South Carolina, on March 15, 1994. Mother and Harold were planning a four-day trip to the annual country music fest at Mountain View, Arkansas, on April 14, 1994 through April 16, 1994. Shown on the following pages are two photos of our trip to Mountain View, Arkansas, with Mother and Harold. The first photo, photograph 17, consists of top photo, of Mother and Janneth behind their motorhome at Mountain View. The bottom photo shows me and Janneth, Harold with his back to camera, and Martha and her husband in background. The second photo, photograph 18, consists of top photo, with from left Harold Craig, Betty Cartwright, her husband Ed Cartwright sitting with his guitar, Janneth, Mother, and Floyd Craig. The middle photo, shows Janneth and Ed

60

Cartwright. The bottom photo consists of many friends of Harold and Mother with Janneth and includes Ed and Betty Cartwright, Martha and her husband Walter, Floyd Craig and others.

We returned to Memphis on April 13, 1994, and followed them to Mountain View, Arkansas. Mother and Harold had a motor home and Harold's brother, Floyd Craig, was going and would be staying with them in their motor home. We took our conversion van, and planned to sleep in it. It was an excellent trip with the fellowship of Mother, Harold, and their friends.

When I started writing to Janneth in early 1993 and pledged to try to get her to marry me, I enrolled in a free urology medical study sponsored by a pharmaceutical company while working and living in Tampa. I have never smoked (cigarettes, cigars, or anything) in my life. I have drank some beer; however I quit drinking beer in March 1993 when I applied for Janneth's visa. I wanted to find

out from the blood chemistry, the nine EKG's that were run monthly that my heart was normal. And the study indicated that I was in good health. Janneth missed her April 1994 menstrual cycle. When she missed again in May and started having some vomiting in morning, we went to the Spartanburg Health Department on Friday, May 25, 1994. We found out she was pregnant! This was one of the joyous moments for God blessing us. And our daughter,

Dorothy Love Sanders, was born in December 1994. Thus, when we found out Janneth was going to have a baby, we realized Jesus Christ was carrying us in his footsteps. I prayed that God would Bless Janneth and our expectant baby as "by God's grace, God was fulfilling His plan for our lives."

We immediately wired Janneth's Mom, Juanita Emberador and Father, Tony Emberador. We told them that Janneth was going to have a baby. We also called Mother and Harold and told them that Janneth was going to have a baby. Here, we were going to have a baby, and I still didn't have a job. One week earlier, Chris, one of the managers at Piccadilly Cafeteria in Westgate Mall in Spartanburg had hired Janneth at $4.50 per hour to work in Salads and Hot Foods on the cafeteria serving line. It was Janneth's first job in America. Janneth did not know how to drive an automobile, and she was working part-time with four hours in evenings and eight hours on Saturday or Sundays. And Janneth worked until several months before Dorothy Love (I called her Dot Love as that's what some nicknamed my mother) was born. In October 4, 1994, I got a job with Aide Design Engineers, Greenville, South Carolina, on a two-year contract assignment located at Engelhard Corporation in Seneca, South Carolina. I was going to have to commute to Clemson and Seneca daily and drive almost 150 miles a day for the next two years. This employment contract with Aide Design Engineers on the Engelhard Corp. contract lasted for two years.

RELIGIOUS EXPERIENCES AND SPIRITUAL GROWTH THROUGH THE FELLOWSHIP OF BROTHERS AND SISTERS IN CHRIST

Shown on following pages is photo of Janneth's parents, <u>photograph 19, which</u> <u>shows from left Juanita Emberador, her Mother, Antonio Emberador, Janneth's Father,</u> <u>Janneth and Dorothy Love in center.</u> That the first Sunday approximately, March 21, 1994, after we got back from Telluride and Memphis, that Sunday we decided to go to Westgate Baptist Church which was close by Oak Forest in Spartanburg Westside. The pastor was Edward Deese; Pastor Deese was an excellent preacher of God's Word. We got a card from Mr. and Mrs. Jim Smith after our first Sunday visit and continued going back to Westgate for over a year. Pastor Ed Deese, baptized me the second Sunday in that December 18, 1994. This was a couple of weeks before Dot Love was born. Pastor Deese recommended that the church sisters in Christ give Janneth a baby shower after Dorothy Love had arrived. Shown below are the photographs of that baby shower at Westgate Baptist Church. In the <u>photograph 20, which consists of three photos: the top photos</u> <u>shows from left Janneth, Pastor Deese's wife and another sister in Christ. The middle</u>

photo shows Janneth opening presents and Assistant Pastor's wife Pat holding Dorothy Love; and the bottom photo shows from left Janneth, Mrs Smith, Pastor Deese's wife and another sister in Christ.

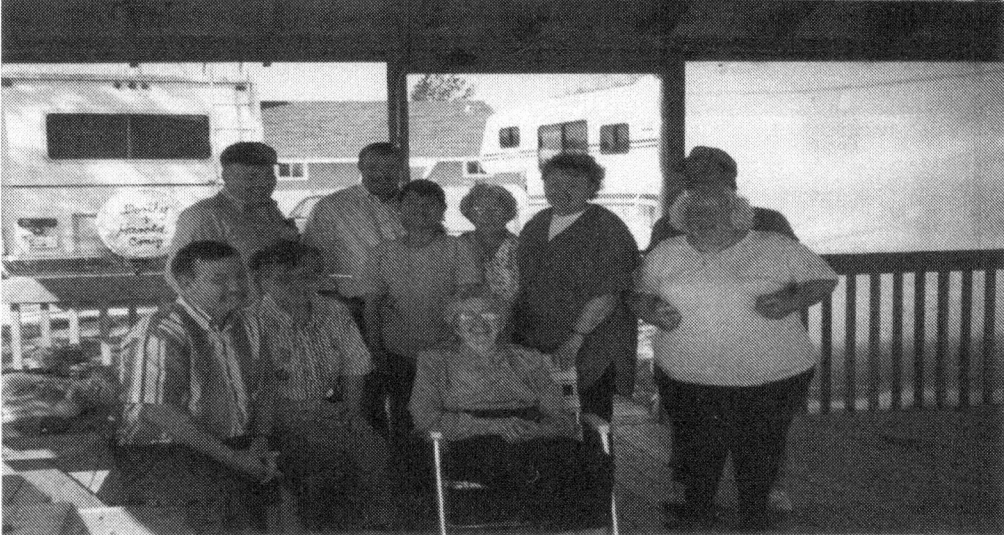

I was baptized in the Presbyterian Church in Raleigh, Tennessee, as a teenager. My Mother, sister and brother and I were founding members of Raleigh Presbyterian Church in Raleigh, Tennessee. I always remember my first romance with Jesus Christ "my first Love" as it is the foundation for which I was raised. I remember My Father didn't go to church with us that often. He drank and smoked cigarettes since he had been a small boy in Crockett Mills, Tennessee.

The corrupt Doctor Charles Jarrett in Methodist Hospital North at Raleigh, Tennessee, (Austin Peay Highway) gave my Father huge dosages of Heparin in that June 7, 1982. Doctor Charles Jarrett of Methodist Hospital North at Raleigh, Tennessee, caused my father to suffer a severe massive heart failure in less than forty hours. My father never had any history of heart trouble, but my father did have bleeding stomach ulcers and was medically discharged from the U.S. Army in 1946. He was discharged for his bleeding ulcers. The U. S. Army had diagnosed him with bleeding ulcers, and that he went to Nashville annually to review his medical conditions. I was working in Birmingham, Alabama, at the time in June 7, 1982, when my father suffered a stroke. I realize today that God is, and God is always in control. However in June 7, 1982, I will forever hold Dr. Charles Jarrett criminally responsible. As my father had seen Dr. Charles Jarrett several times and Jarrett was aware, had my father's medical records from the U.S. Army. Heparin is a blood thinner and is a very dangerous blood thinner. The bombastic, negligent, carelessness, neglect and pompous Dr. Charlie Jarrett criminally caused my father's death. When you have a person that has bleeding ulcers, you don't give that patient any blood thinners. My father was not in a life-threatening situation until this stupid, plain dumb Dr. Charles Jarrett gave him Heparin, and caused major heart failure. On the first night I got there to see him, they were pumping, aspirating out more fluids than they were administering to him. Dr. Charles Jarrett was criminally negligent; however he was not punished! My father's bleeding so many fluids resulted in his heart being massively overloaded by all the fluid pressure. For the proper medical treatment would have been to not administer any fluids into him. Proper medical treatment would have been to closely monitor. Since Jarrett knew of his bleeding ulcers and had his U. S. Army records, Dr. Jarrett was criminally negligent! {You should not be giving a patient, who for forty years has had history of bleeding stomach ulcers, the dangerous drug, Heparin; and as matter of medicine technology, a much safer blood thinner would have been Cumene, if they administered anything}

After Daddy died, I signed affidavit requesting all medical records from Methodist Hospital North. The bombastic, negligent, carelessness, neglect and pompous Dr. Charlie Jarrett has not ever been punished nor disciplined. The office manager for Methodist Hospital North was Jim Pickle, who was in my Bartlett High School, Bartlett, Tennessee graduating class. For these medical records showed that my father lost some 5000 cc of fluids, whereas they only gave him some 2750 cc of fluids. That Doctor Charles Jarrett and the entire Methodist Hospital North criminally felony murdered my father.

I wasn't interested in obtaining money, as revenge is with our Lord. I wanted an attorney to get a case to trial before a jury. I wanted full depositions and cross examination of Dr. Charles Jarrett. I wanted Dr. Charles Jarrett to feel my pain when he got off the witness stand. wanted a full apology for his negligence and for the Methodist

North Hospital to institute new medical provisions and medical competence, new doctors and whatever else was required to prevent any other stupid, incompetent, other doctor administering Heparin to a patient who had had bleeding ulcers for forty years. I wanted the Tennessee Medical Board to pull Dr. Charles Jarrett's license. I wanted him to be deprived of possibly murdering another's loved one. The Methodist Hospital North should have already had these safeguards; however they didn't! I paid the attorney fees and paid the filing fees for Mother to file in Shelby County Courts system. My Mother eventually dropped the suit, probably on recommendations

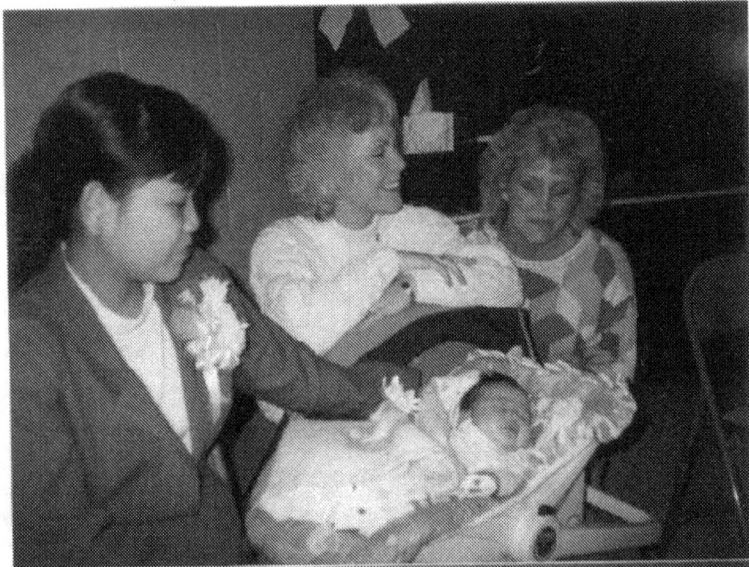

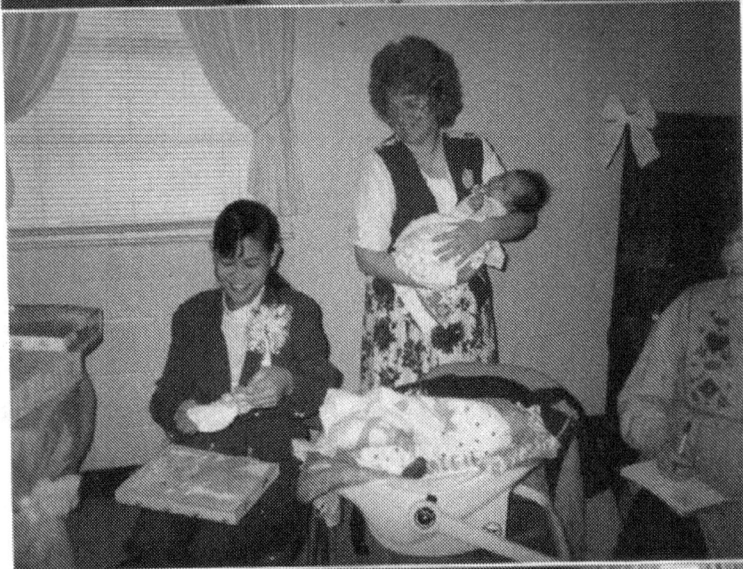

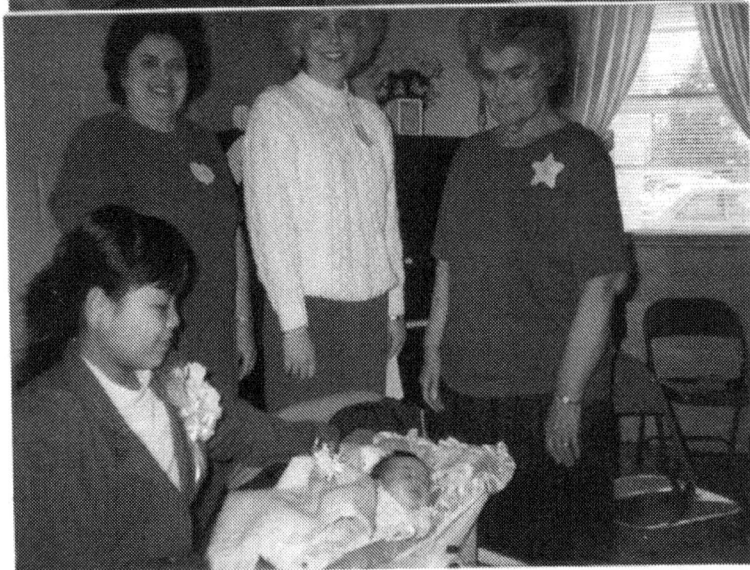

from my sister and didn't proceed.

In the photograph on preceding page is <u>photograph 21, which shows my biological Mother and father, Dorothy Love Sanders and Aaron Sanders Jr.</u> My brother and sister thought that all these doctors were like God. I did not. There is a song by "Mike and the Mechanics" titled "<u>The Living Years</u>". In this song you should tell all your loved ones in the living years how much you love them! I truly felt that I had not told my father enough times in this earthly world how much I really loved him. Another verse in the song that I truly adhere to is the verse "Thought I saw his image in my newborn's tears when she was born!" And you know when Dot Love was born that day in December 1994, I thought I saw my Daddy's image and facial expressions in Dorothy Love (Dot Love) Sanders. I truly know all children are gifts from God, and I am thankful the Lord blessed Janneth and me with this gift from God. We are a Godly family serving the Lord. We truly know God has given us and blessed us with two children who are on loan from Him!

For after my father was murdered, I paid for an attorney for Mother on behalf of my father's estate and sued Dr. Charlie Jarrett and Methodist Hospital North. This was my first experience with corrupt doctors and attorneys. The attorneys would tell you that your father was 62 years old, and in Tennessee it was very difficult to prove damages. If it was a younger person in his twenty's, then the State and State laws looked at it very differently. The state looked at monetary damages to provide treatment costs, and other medical for rest of their life in this earthly world. One of the attorneys mentioned to me "Well, your father has lived a good life and was 62 years old." I thought you could get equitable relief in Tennessee's and America's Courts. But you can never, ever achieve that. Recent killing of our children by children in our schools (Littleton, Colorado, and the Jewish Academy in Los Angeles most recent) show that God has been thrown out of our schools. When I was running for Congress in 1998, one of the radio stations in Columbia, South Carolina, cut me off the air when I stated my views that prayer should be put back into the schools. Just recently, I read in the Sunday newspaper that Eric Harris and Dylan Klebold's diaries were released to the public. They both were devout racists! Derived from their diaries were their profanities throughout their writings; and they both were lost and didn't know God. I wrote this in 1999 when I first started writing my biography: "I do believe some day soon we must have an evangelical revival restoring God's way into our earthly world life." It's like Bill Maher mentioned one night talking about Columbine. He stated "that Klebold and Eric Harris drove their BMW's to Columbine that morning." Yes, the parents have failed also as they have not led their own lives following the footsteps of Jesus Christ. If they had led their earthly lives as saviors of Jesus Christ and by the grace of God, their two children and the other 13 killed, murdered students and teachers might well be alive in this earthly world. And Pastor Michael Hamlet, Pastor of First Baptist North Spartanburg, in one of his Sunday sermons from God's Word just before our June 8, 1998, debate at Greenville Tech "stated it was the acts of the devil. That America had lost sight of what this country was founded." And that as the Bible tells us we can do nothing without the Lord. "We are all sinners and we have to trust in the Lord. We have to repent and accept Jesus Christ as our personal savior, and are anew in Christ. We have to turn ourselves away from sin and have that true almighty fine relationship and walk with Jesus Christ".

For just last night I watched the NBC ER's episode called "Fight the Good Fight."

"In this episode a father (named Nelson) and his daughter were hit by van in auto accident. The daughter had the most severe injuries. Since the father had kidnapped the daughter from the mother in Cleveland, the father left the hospital. In this episode the doctor (I believe played by Noah Wiley), and the resident named Lucy spent most of show trying to find the father, Nelson. The daughter had to have blood transfusions prior to surgery and of course in the script, he was the only one with matched blood type! The African American surgeon during one of exams mentioned 'Heparin flush.' This dialogue by the writers was highly unethical and inaccurate." Heparin is a very dangerous drug (a blood thinner) that can cause various patients to bleed to death. And it may lead to congestive heart failures even though they may have no histories of heart failure. "At end of the show Noah Wiley put his arms around Lucy

and told her she had fought the good fight!" But you know the good fight is to be like Moses. We have to learn that no matter how many trials and tribulations we go through in this earthly world, just as God let Moses tarry in that wilderness for forty years on the other side of the desert until he knew Moses was ready to lead the chosen out of bondage from the Egyptians. Moses, just like all of us, had to learn "everything I do, I do for the power, glory and glorification of God." Faith in Jesus Christ, walking with Jesus Christ and bearing the Holy Spirit within our hearts is what it is all about in this earthly world.

After Westgate Baptist we visited both Grace Bible Church in September, October, and November 1996 and First Baptist North Spartanburg Church on several occasions. At Grace Bible Church the pastor was Eric Sipe. Grace Bible Church was meeting in rented spaces on Blackstock Road in Spartanburg and had plans to build a church on Highway 290 in Moore. I believe their church was completed on Highway 290 in Duncan sometime in 1998. Janneth, Dot Love, and I had lunch on several occasions following Sunday worship with Leonard and Barbara Waterman and their daughter. Barbara Waterman had been a missionary in the Philippines for several years before she and Leonard got married. One of Janneth's goals is to become a missionary and go back to Philippines and witness for Christ and bring people to the Lord. The Philippine people, as I have mentioned, have strong family ties and foundations. They daily visit their family and neighbors and always support their families. It is a shame that some in America have really lost this focus on God, family and country! I know as when in early 1998 when Janneth was studying the 150 questions for her Naturalization as U.S. Citizen, she put forth great efforts. Janneth got all her questions right before the U.S. Immigration and Naturalization Examiner during the Oral Exam in March 1998. And on June 5, 1998, she along with 81 other immigrants were sworn in by Honorable U.S. District Judge William Traxler at the same U.S, Federal Courthouse, Haynesworth Courthouse, corner Washington and Church Streets, in Greenville, South Carolina. This is where I have so many bad memories of the corrupt federal justice system. And there's another bias, pompous, extremely prejudiced U.S. Magistrate named Bucky Catoe, who never lets Pro Se litigants access the system. I do believe Judge William Traxler has been nominated to the U.S. 4th Circuit Appeals Court; thank God it wasn't Henry Herlong.

We also visited First Baptist North Spartanburg and received several calls from one of the adult Sunday school teachers Mrs. Debra Gosnell. The First Baptist North Spartanburg is a large God fearing family of Christians. This was the latter part of 1996, and later in February 1998, I joined the Church. We attended the Sunday School class that Debra Gosnell taught. Debra Gosnell and husband, Don Gosnell, are God-fearing Christians. Debra Gosnell later became Dorothy's third grade teacher at Cooley Springs Fingerville Elementary School. I yearned to go every Sunday morning to hear Debra Gosnell and Matt Henderson deliver the Sunday School message. Matt Henderson is a combat Vietnam Veteran. The Sunday morning he was giving testimony to his witnessing for Christ and describing his Vietnam experience and his service for our country was awesome! It was a great experience in my life. And I still miss and love all my brothers and sisters in Christ at First Baptist North Spartanburg including all the ministers and Pastor Michael Hamlet. Pastor Michael Hamlet has God in his heart and delivers the message and word from the heart. I remember a lot of messages Pastor Hamlet delivered. One Sunday after Frank Sinatra died, he used the analogy of one of his songs "I did it all on my own, I did it my own way!" Of course, Pastor Hamlet was truly inspired from

God's holy word. "It's all about your faith in Jesus Christ our savior, to publicly accept Jesus Christ as your personal savior, repent, turn away from the old and be anew in Christ. It's about the blood of Christ as Christ was crucified, dead, and buried, and the third day arose from the dead to live among us. Jesus Christ is Lord and is the Holy Spirit who lives in each of our hearts. Only Jesus Christ, the Son of God, has risen! Christ is the only one raised from the dead. What Pastor Hamlet was detailing was that you can never, ever do it on your own; you cannot do it your own way. You can only do it through Jesus Christ, our Personal Savior. Repent and accept Christ as your savior; be born again!" Again, don't fear death as "to live is Christ and to die is gain." You cannot do it by one or alone. You have to be in Christ, and only Jesus Christ, the Holy Spirit, will through our Holy Absolute Father, grant you the power in this earthly world. God Bless all my brothers and sisters in Christ! And Pastor Hamlet is right! As if you think you can do it your own way, do it your way, "then you are lost and do not know God." Only by trusting in Christ may you serve the Lord and commune with Jesus Christ daily.

That in January 1997 Janneth accepted a job with Springs Industries Inc., Lyman, South Carolina, as a Quality Control Inspector. David Mack worked in the Color Department at Springs Industries. Janneth and I had dinner with David Mack and his wife Mary Mack and their children on several occasions. David Mack was a deacon at Paramount Park Baptist Church in Greenville and had invited us to his church. David Mack and Mary Mack are Godly Christians who God guided in our life. We visited David Mack's church the very next Sunday. We joined Paramount Park Baptist Church and continued going for all year of 1997. David Mack attends Tabernacle Baptist College in evenings and is working toward his Pastoral Degree to become a pastor. Paramount

Park Baptist is an African American Church with several Caucasian members, Mary Nell McCall, and Emma Mackey and others. All are Godly Christians serving the Lord!

When Janneth was sworn in at the U.S. Federal Courthouse on Friday, June 5, 1998, in Greenville, South Carolina, I was a candidate for the U.S. Congress. I was not able to get the local TV stations to cover the swearing in of these eighty-two, 82, immigrant Americans in their U.S. Naturalization ceremony. I did thoroughly enjoy the Christian fellowship at Paramount Park Baptist Church. Pastor of the church was Bobby Randolph. Assistant Pastor was William Thompson. Pastor Randolph and many of the Congregation had many years earlier started a Bible Study Group in Paramount Park. Two of the deacons are David Mack and Tony Jones. If you are ever in Greenville, you may wish to worship the Lord at Paramount Park Baptist Church on Augusta Road in Greenville. Just six months earlier in June 1996 Paramount Park Baptist had the opportunity to purchase the former Bible Presbyterian Church on Augusta Road, just down from intersection of Augusta Road and Academy Street. The church is a beautiful house of the Lord built back in the early days of Greenville's existence. One of the church members is life-long residence of Greenville's Westside and also a founding member of the former Bible Presbyterian, Christian Ms Emma Mackey. Ms Mackey is 86 years old. She loves to tell the story of when she brought a six-year-old Greenville Jewish boy to Christ. One of Ms. Mackey's friends who picked her up to give her a ride to church was Mrs .Mary Nell Mccall.

Janneth, Dot Love and I have invited Ms Emma Mackey to our house on several occasions to lunch and dinner. Ms Mackey is in a nursing home currently, and we pray for her (this was written in 1999). The Lord called Ms Emma Mackey home to the Lord in 2004. I told her during the Congressional campaign that I wanted her to do an advertisement with us. However, we never got enough money to achieve that goal.

I always remember one of the credence's of Pastor Bobby Randolph, "You have to be founded, grounded and rooted up in the word of the Lord!" And you know, Pastor Randolph is a genuine person of God. Paramount Park Baptist Church in Greenville, South Carolina, is a church that really cares about you. During 1997 and 1998 we attended Paramount Park. One of the most vivid dreams I had was after Assistant Pastor Thompson preached one of his sermons in Revelations. After this vision, I awoke up Janneth and asked her to pray with me. It was 3:30 A.M. in the morning. I believe God was sending me a spiritual message in this vision. A second vivid dream I had, I believe, was another spiritual message. This dream was so vivid in that it seemed in reality that I awoke up twice from this dream. This dream seemed so vivid that all during the dream you wanted to wake up and prove it was just a dream. I awoke from the dream, and promised God if I made any money from my wastewater patent that I would give it all to evangelism ministries. Janneth wants to become a missionary to the Philippines. (1999 when I wrote this) "Whatever God's plan is for me, I am going to continue praying for God to lead me in that righteous path. Jesus Christ can carry me across the river in guiding me in what is God's plan." In my third dream I will share some of what I remember, "It seemed like there was a birthday party for me. In the dream I remember commenting to someone "That's the Best Birthday party I've ever had!" Secondly, I evidently was involved in making this movie, and someone commented we did a good job. And it seemed like I knew some of people in this dream; however I don't specifically remember anyone. I do plan to keep my promise to the Lord in my walk with Christ.

Pastor Bobby Randolph in 1997 was still teaching at Tri-County Tech, and in later 1997 retired from Tri-County Tech to devote full time to Ministering at Paramount Park Baptist Church. The Times ran a very splendid article, pictures on his retirement ceremony at Tri- County Tech.

Janneth, Dot Love, and I went to Paramount Park for over a year. Rachel Moore was a student at Bob Jones University. On Sunday in August 1997 when Rachel's Mother and Dad accompanied her back to Bob Jones for start of the school year, they sang a trio "I was raised in Sunday School and Church!" I have their trio on tape as I was videotaping that Sunday morning. There were a lot of tears after their Christian song that Sunday morning. Christ lives in Paramount Park Baptist Church on Augusta road in Greenville, South Carolina. There are many good singers at this Church including Pastor Bobby Randolph and his wife Maybelle Randolph, who has been a schoolteacher for over 25 years. The "Singing Gospel Echos" who consist of several sisters of the church are extremely inspiring. I loved to hear them sing Sunday mornings at Paramount; I really miss all God's love and fellowship at Paramount Park Baptist Church. Assistant Pastor Willie Thompson is manager of the Greenville Christian radio station 94.5 WMUU on Wade Hampton Boulevard next to Bob Jones University. He teaches at Bob Jones University. Pastor Thompson and his wife are also gorgeous, inspiring, singers. Many Sundays they have performed duets. Pastor Randolph is a great, spiritual singer and on some mornings "that the Lord had bear on his heart to sing one of his favorite Christian hymns," he would sing that Lord inspired hymn. Paramount Park Baptist Church is filled with brothers and sisters in Christ. It is a church that cares about you. I pray that anytime you may be in the upstate Greenville, South Carolina, area that you might visit

Paramount Park Baptist Church. That you might experience for yourselves the living spirit 'the fruit of the spirit" of Jesus Christ in the hearts of all at Paramount Park Baptist Church.

The photo on the following pages was taken at Paramount Park Baptist Church on Augusta Road, Greenville, South Carolina. This photo, photograph 22, consists of the following: top photo, from left Mrs. Emma Mackey in pink coat holding Dorothy Love's hand, back row Kimberly Mack, Mary Mack, Launeil, Deacon Tony Jones and Tony Jones' son. Bottom photo, shows Mrs. Emma Mackey holding Dorothy Love's hand.

Another lady, a God-fearing Christian whom God has guided into my life is Eunice Wilson. Dorothy Love, Colonel Sanders and I went to her sister, Clementine Thomas' funeral yesterday July 28, 2006, at Jerusalem Baptist Church in Jonesville South Carolina. Eunice Wilson's sister has been called home to be with our Lord. As God has prepared mansions for us in Heaven in our Lord's House, are we ready to go meet our Heavenly Father in His House? In 1 Corinthians Chapter 15:51-58 God describes' "the Christian's Victory Through Christ." 51) "What God is saying the 'rapture' of the church described in these verses were a mystery unknown in the Old Testament, but now revealed. We shall not all sleep, not all die. Some will be alive when the Lord returns, but all will be changed. 56) The sting of death is sin because it is by sin that death gains authority over man, and the strength of sin is the law, because the law stirs up sin (also Romans 5:12, Romans 7:8-11) 58) A firm belief in the resurrection and a solid hope for the future gives incentive for service in the present."

After my spouse died in 1990, Eunice Wilson became a very good friend and sister in Christ. I shared with Eunice some of my trials, and shared with her Janneth. I knew God had sent me the Christian lady of my life, in Janneth Emberador! Eunice Wilson was invited to our wedding, but couldn't come all the way to Tennessee at that time. After Janneth gave birth to Dorothy Love Sanders in that December 1994, Eunice came over to help Janneth and the baby. I was driving 150 miles a day back and forth to Seneca, South Carolina, on the Engelhard job. Eunice, praise God for you, a child of God and a sister in Christ. You have my 'agape love' that began with God. I am a Christian and praise God that you Eunice will be raptured with me to our Heavenly Father's house to sit on the right hand of God the Father Almighty. Thank you, Eunice, and thank God he brought you, a sister in Christ, into my life in the time of God's plan, his Plan! God is in Control!

We joined Oak Grove Baptist Church in the Westgate area. As long as God let's me live in this earthly world, I will have on my heart the sermon message that Pastor Cheneyworth had on his heart and delivered September 9,2001, "*Thirty Minutes and Counting.*" God had evidently laid on Pastor Cheneyworth's heart to preach this message without unfolding to the pastor what was to happen in America two days in the future. As in even God revealing to Pastor Cheneyworth in that September 9, 2001, I believe God wants us to do more and lead more lost souls to Christ. {Chapter 18 Create 2,500,000 Disciples of America during a Co-Presidency

Campaign and in Chapter 19 America Is Ready.} Our Sunday school teacher was Mark Line, who, I believe, is Athletic Director at Wofford College here in Spartanburg, South Carolina. Mrs. Betty Bridges (who plays the piano and organ), her husband, Jerry Bridges and Mrs. Chaneyworth came over for Christian fellowship at the rental town home we were living in at that time. They shared Christian fellowship with us; and I praise God for these Christian disciples who came into our life and remain in our lives.

On the preceding page is the photo of Thien Pham and his family; photograph 23, consists of the following: top photo, from left Langiene , Thien Pham's daughter, Dorothy Love and David, Thien Pham's son; middle photo from left, Thien Pham , Langiene, Launeil, David, and Thien Pham's wife Naw and Dorothy Love in high chair. Bottom photo consists from left Naw , Dorothy Love, Langiene and Janneth.

And after we moved to the Fingerville and North Boiling Springs area we joined New Prospect Baptist Church. Janneth worked with John Griffin who was a Supervisor at Springs Industries Inc. John and and his wife Kathy Griffin were members of New Prospect Baptist Church. Dr. Ron Gaddy is the pastor; Pastor David Tate is the Youth and Outreach Minister and Vicky White is the Church Secretary who has helped me many times. I thank Vicky for her kind, courteous, generous help in my walks with Christ and in assisting me in computer operations in the times I needed to borrow some computer time!

We joined James Justice's "Honor the Master Sunday School class"; I also became James Justice's alternate teacher and taught the class on times when James could not teach or be present. James and Karen Justice are Godly brothers and sisters in Christ and their Christian daughter, Sierra, became close Christian friends. Thank God for you James and Karen for inviting Dorothy to travel with your family on the many Christian outings and ventures. Dorothy truly benefited from your family's Christian agape love. Our Honor the Master class consisted of James and Karen Justice, Lynn and David

Baldwin, Huey and Teri Hicks, Norm and Kim Ilderton, Billy Hart, Lethia Ford, Sheri

Mathis, Sherri and M.C. Martin, Terry and Kim Martin, Beverly and Warren O'Sullivan,

Pat and Terri Phillips, Tina and Ervin Reid, Janneth and I, Bob and Alison White and

Chip and Mary Kay Wilson. Ms. Lorraine Green and Margie Giles are Godly sisters in

Christ and teachers who are committing their lives to Christ 24/7, daily in the continuous

service! God Bless you Lorraine and Margie! I know the night before John Griffin was

scheduled to have his cancer surgery, Pastor Gaddy and all the deacons went over to

Kathy and John Griffin's house for prayer together. I know that Dr. Gaddy, the deacons,

and the rest of the ministry prayer group administered the anointment of the healing

hands of prayer and Christ upon John Griffin and others. I don't know of John Griffin's

current medical status; however I believe God still has John in the Plan he had for him.

Since John Griffin worked with Janneth at Springs Industries Inc. for the seven years,

John knows the moral fiber of my wife, Janneth Sanders.

In July 2006, we joined Boiling Springs First Baptist Church, Boiling

Springs, South Carolina. Dr.Hank Williams is the Senior Pastor, Carlton Berry is the

Associate Pastor, Jason Waters is the Minister of Students, Keith Higginbotham is the

Minister of Senior Adults (and Keith also performs tremendously in the church's Upward

Basketball programs for the youth and children) and Ann Collins is the Director of

Children's Ministries. Dr. Hank Williams, who I believe has served in evangelism all

around the world, is an extremely efficient deliverer of God's word. Some of these

sermons that Pastor Hank preached on this summer that were titled "Fruit of The Spirit",

I felt inspired to share with you! Janneth and I joined the Cornerstone Sunday School

class. Since joining last July 2006, Janneth and I have shared some of the Philippines

Asian chicken, shrimp, pork, panzit food delicacies prior to our morning class. The Cornerstone Class has four teachers who deliver the word of God! And they are all awesome, astounding as it seems the Sunday School class only lasts only about five minutes. These four teachers are Gary Brown, Paul Bleckley, Larry Lawter and Eddie Cole. If you live in the Spartanburg District Two, Boiling Springs, visit our church. We will share that nurtured spirit of Christ with you! Boiling Springs First Baptist Church truly is "A Church with a Passion for Christ and a Passion for People." Pastor Hank has challenged Janneth and I to pray cessantly about leading a mission trip to the Cebu, Philippines the summer of 2008. Boiling Springs First Baptist Church website is as follows: www.bsfbc.org

The members of our Cornerstone Sunday School class are as follows: Mrs. Patty Allen, Mr. Rich Allen, Mr. Paul Bleckley, Mrs. Ruth Ann Brooks, Mr. Gary Brown, Mrs. Becky Brown, Mr. Arden Camp, Mrs. Elise Camp, Mrs. Beth Charles, Mr. Leslie Charles, Mrs. June Childers, Mr. Keith Childers, Mr. Eddie Cole, Mrs. Peggy Cole, Mr. Mark Cramer, Mrs. Tammy Cramer, Mrs. Sharon Gilstrap, Mr. Stanley Gilstrap, Mr. Ligon Henderson, Mrs. Rhonda Henderson, Mrs. Kathy Lawter, Mr. Larry Lawter, Mrs. Ann Lowe, Mr. Ronnie Lowe, Mrs Karen Mathis, Mr. Wally Mathis, Mr. Durwood Merritt, Mrs. Elaine Merritt, Mrs. Sandra O'Bryant, Mr. Jack O'Bryant, Mrs. Rita Parker, Mr. Steve Parker, Mrs. Janneth Sanders, and I, Launeil Neil Sanders, Mr. David Scruggs, Mrs. Diane Scruggs, Mrs. Patsy Trout, Mr. Robert Trout, Mr. Joe Williams, Mrs. Judy Williams, Mr. Kenneth Williams, Mrs. Joy Williams and Mrs. Beatrice Wofford.

Some of our closest Christian friends are Andy and Jean Bartley and their son Corbin of Laurens, South Carolina. Andy and Jenny are devout Christians, and we have attended their church in Laurens, South Carolina, on specific homecomings, and they have visited New Prospect Baptist Church with us on several occasions. Andy and Jenny have been attempting to complete their international adoption of a Philippines daughter, however they have experienced many difficulties and obstacles from the U.S. Citizenship and Immigration Service and the Homeland Security investigative agency.

Shown is the photo of Andy Bartley and family, photograph 24, which consists of the following: from left their adopted daughter from Philippines, Andy's wife Jenny, Andy Bartley and with Andy holding his and Jenny's son, Corbin.

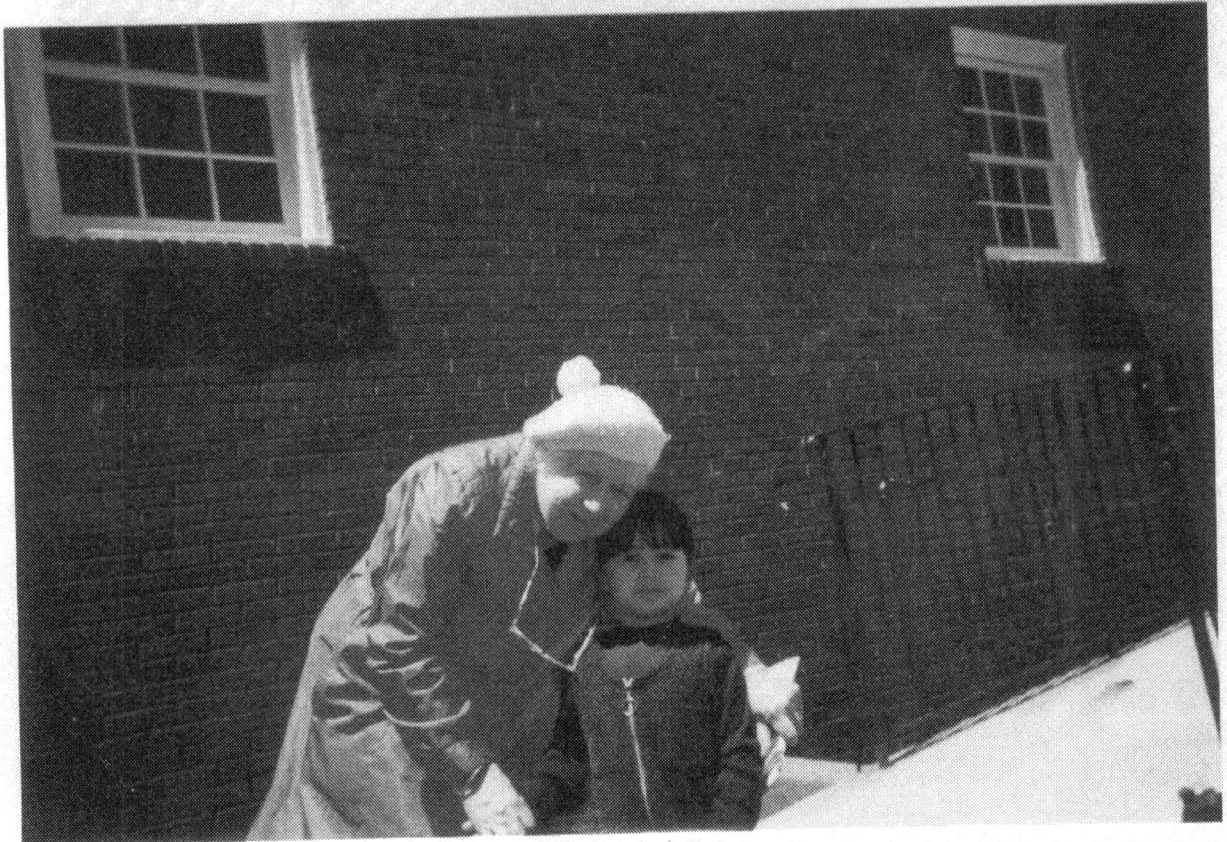

8

LAUNEIL NEIL SANDERS AND JANNETH EMBERADOR SANDERS HAVE DAUGHTER DOROTHY LOVE (DOT LOVE) SANDERS AND SON COLONEL LAUNEIL TONY SANDERS

<u>Birth of our Daughter, Dorothy Love Sanders:</u> Earlier we discovered from Spartanburg Regional Health Department on May 25, 2004, that Janneth was pregnant. I knew I was going to be a father again. I felt the Lord had answered my prayers and had blessed us. I truly believe all children are gifts from God. God was blessing us. During nine months, God was having Jesus Christ walk with us.

The first week of July 1994 on a Tuesday, Janneth wanted to go fishing. We drove down to Charleston, South Carolina. We paid for a day trip boat out from Charleston harbor for deep-sea fishing. I should have known better, however she wanted to go fishing. I really didn't think about how sick this might make her in her pregnancy state. I was extremely happy about Janneth being pregnant, and knew we both wanted a baby. We paid the money for the two adults for the day trip. Remember, in the Philippines her native town is right on the ocean, and she can buy fresh ocean fish at the market daily. It seemed we left the harbor around 7:30 A.M. that morning. I believe we went about 35 miles off shore. Only after maybe 10 miles off shore, Janneth got sick. She was sick for most of the sea fishing trip. I knew I had made a terrible mistake, and I prayed to God that he prevent Janneth from having any miscarriage or other medical condition that would result in us losing the baby. I had used bad judgment in us going out to sea during these nine months. But I wanted to please Janneth. We did buy some of the red snapper that was caught on our deep-sea fishing trip; and we drove back to Spartanburg, South Carolina, and cooked our red snapper. We also went by the Charleston fresh fish market and bought more shrimp, fish and seafood to bring back with us.

The next week we went to Atoka, Tennessee, to visit with Mother and Harold for a few days. During this trip we told Mother if it were a girl, we planned to name the baby Dorothy Love Sanders, after her. And of which we eventually did; and it wasn't until September 1994 that the doctor scheduled the ultrasound, that it revealed that the baby was going to be a girl! We then could see the images that it was a girl. We saved the ultrasound printout in our photograph album somewhere. I didn't find out until after delivery in December 1994 that Janneth didn't totally trust the ultrasound! Mother acted very proud that we were going to name our baby after her.

In August 1994 I accepted an interview trip to New York City, New York, to interview with a South Korean steel company. I wanted Janneth to see part of the Atlantic coast states and to get to visit New York City. We went to lunch at the Carnegie Deli on upper Broadway one afternoon. Prices had increased by almost 200% in past ten years as now in August 1994 the price of the Pastrami sandwich was $19.00 compared to $7.50

ten years earlier. I wasn't successful in obtaining the contract assignment, but Janneth and I got to share together our trip to New York City.

When we got back from New York City, I received an inquiry in an environmental contract position with Aide Design Engineers Inc, Greenville, South Carolina. The position was a contract environmental engineer position with one of their clients, Engelhard Corporation in Seneca, South Carolina. Even though I was now going to drive 150 miles round trip a day, I now had a contract job. Before I got the position I had to drive down to Engelhard Corporation and interview with Rodney Kutz and other officials for personal interviews and approval. And as stated I worked on this Aide Design Engineers Inc contract for two years as detailed in other chapter of this biography.

So we went into the Spartanburg Regional Medical Center on Christmas Eve on that December 24, 1994; however the medical intern told us it was not quite time. They sent us back home. Then we returned on Christmas night on that December 25, 1994, and they induced labor and Dorothy Love was born. I got to hold Dot Love first after they cleaned her up on the stainless delivery tray. Janneth was gleaming, and I did videotape the birth.

Birth of Our Son, Colonel Launeil Tony Sanders:

Since Janneth obtained her U.S. Naturalization in June 1998, it took almost three years to obtain the visa approval for her parents. Her parents arrived in America on January 16, 2001. We had sold our house in Oak Forest subdivision so that my children from my marriage to Evelyn could obtain their money. We rented a three-bedroom town home in Canaan Pointe estates. I kept thinking I might be able to get decent paying job again, and it might require relocation. Canaan Pointe Town homes had a lot of problems, and even before we moved into our home in Fingerville that we built; there were severe crime problems.

As you look in the Bible in Ruth as quoted in the last chapter of my biography, you see God granted conception to Ruth in her second marriage Ruth had been childless in her first marriage to Mahlon, but God gave Ruth the reward, a husband in Boaz and gave her conception through Boaz and the son. Since Janneth thought my daughter is 8 ½ years old my husband is too old, I probably can't have any more children. We consummated God's "agape love," and God proved He is in control that Sunday afternoon in September 2002. God granted conception to Mary, a Virgin, as she had never been with a man. Isn't it so awesome, astounding to visualize the almighty power, glory, and prestige of our Almighty Holy Father?

Since Janneth's parents had had three daughters, I prayed that this baby would be a son! I knew that I could have a son as God blessed my former spouse, Evelyn, and I with a son, Aaron Neil Sanders. So Dorothy Love, Janneth's parents and I were praying at the ultrasound day that God would let it be a boy. I detailed earlier that Janneth's parents live with us. Since Mother had come from Tennessee in June 3, 2003, she was present for Colonel Launeil Tony's birth some seven days later. I accepted an assignment located at Engelhard Corporation in Seneca, South Carolina. I was going to have to commute to Clemson and Seneca daily and drive almost 150 miles a day for the next two years. This employment contract with Aide Design Engineers on the Engelhard Corp. contract lasted for two years.

Shown on following page is Colonel Tony Sanders, photograph 25, which consists of our son, pinching Winnie The Pooh's nose!

Shown on following pages is Colonel Tony Sanders, photograph 26, which is our son, Colonel Sanders at approximately three years old.

Shown on following pages is Colonel Tony Sanders, photograph 27, which consists of our son, Colonel Sanders riding and driving his red fire engine.

Shown on photograph 28, on following pages is Colonel Sanders and Dorothy Love Sanders (with her on her knees) holding hands

Shown on photograph 29, on following pages is Colonel Tony Sanders sitting on his red stool

Shown on following pages is Dorothy Love Sanders with her hands on Colonel Tony Sanders' shoulders, photograph 30.

Shown on photograph 31, on following pages is Dorothy Love Sanders at two weeks old in her red dress and Colonel Tony Sanders' at a few weeks old in his blue 45 jump suit

Shown on photograph 32, on following pages is Launeil in Tux standing with Dorothy Love Sanders with the American Flag and balloons!

Shown on following pages is me, Launeil, holding Colonel Tony Sanders' in my lap, photograph 33.

Shown on photograph 34, on following pages is Colonel Tony Sanders in his Batter Up baseball uniform

Shown on photograph 35, on following pages is Launeil reading book to Dorothy Love Sanders. Dorothy is wearing her "Grandma Loves Me Tie Shirt."

Shown on photograph 36, on following pages is Launeil holding Dorothy Love Sanders before the fireplace at Christmas and photo was used in our campaign for Congress.

Shown on photograph 37, on following pages is Colonel Sanders and Dorothy Love Sanders hugging each other!

Shown on photograph 38, on following pages is Dorothy Love Sanders at Ronald McDonald's House

Shown in photograph 40, on following pages is Colonel Tony Sanders at two weeks old wrapped in the American Flag

Shown on photograph 41, on following pages is photo of Janneth , Launeil and Dorothy Love. Top photo is Dorothy Love and Janneth; bottom photo is from top down Janneth, Launeil and Launeil holding Dorothy Love

Shown on photograph 42, on following pages is Colonel Sanders and Dorothy Love Sanders with Colonel Sanders sitting in her lap in the farmhouse

Shown on photograph 43, on following pages is Colonel Tony Sanders sitting on floor holding his blue stool

SENIOR ENVIRONMENTAL ENGINEER POSITION WITH AIDE DESIGN ENGINEERS, GREENVILLE, SOUTH CAROLINA

That on Monday, October 4, 1994, I accepted a position with Aide Design Engineers Inc. in Greenville, South Carolina, for a one year's contract assignment with one of their clients, Engelhard Corporation in Seneca, South Carolina. The contract eventually extended to approximately two years with the last one-half year at a part time rate of approximately 24 hours per week. The contract responsibilities included the performing of engineering calculations from Engelhard's proprietary processes for calculating all emissions to be incorporated into the plant's Title V, Part, 70, Clean Air Act Permit submittal to South Carolina Department of Health & Environmental Control (SCDHEC). These requirements for the Title V, Part 70, Clean Air Act Permit stemmed from the Federal Clean Air Act Amendments of 1990. In the beginning, it was quite apparent that in the original 1987 and 1988 permitting of the Engelhard facility by SCDHEC was flawed. The submittal of air emissions by Engelhard in these permits was inaccurate; the air emissions were incorrect. The engineering emissions performed by Engelhard's Corporate Iselin, New Jersey, offices were grossly inaccurate and never, ever stated the total emissions, that is the Potential To Emit Emissions {PTE} were in error. The reason this is so vitally important is as follows:

That Engelhard Corporation had been cited for environmental violations in the state of New Jersey; and thus, packed up and moved their plant from New Jersey to South Carolina in or around 1988 after SCDHEC approved their permit.

That Engelhard Corporation had been cited for environmental violations in the state of New Jersey; and one who was reasonably knowledgeable about venturi scrubbers, Hydro Sonic Systems (TM, Trademark of Lone Star technologies Inc.) free jet scrubbers, ionizing wet scrubbers (TM-trademark of Ceilkote Inc.) and other state of the art wet scrubbers could quickly see that the three Tri-Mer™ scrubbers (those permitted three wet scrubbers in 1988) were pieces of junk and were not technologically sound. Thus, with the same pieces of junk wet scrubbers that Engelhard had had problems with in New Jersey, they permitted in South Carolina. They packed up all equipment, moved it to Seneca, South Carolina, and re-installed the inadequate, insufficient equipment. These control equipment emitted extreme excesses and thousands of tons of toxic air emissions around Seneca. Many citizens around the surrounding area have developed severe respiratory cancers, and many have died. Those who have contacted these severe terminal respiratory diseases and, or cancers have been deserted by our government.

Pro Se litigants cannot obtain access. You may go to "A Matter of Justice" website, and will find that the hundreds of thousands all across America are denied access. The system seems to be rigged against Pro Se litigants. I heard Bob Lapine of America's "Family Life Today" preaching today on his daily telecast on Blue Ridge Broadcasting Company's radio station. He was preaching on the Godly involvement of you brothers and sisters in Christ in resolving and recovering marital differences to prevent divorces. Again one of his Christian points was that through your church and your brothers and sisters in Christ, you should involve a Christian attorney. Well, in my life over the past sixteen years since my spouse, Evelyn Sanders, died of primary liver cancer, I have only met one Christian attorney. Maybe there are more in America, however my actual experience for the past sixteen years proves there aren't any. If I were President or Co-President of America, I would sign an Executive Order, declaring a National Judicial Emergency, and signifying to all unethical, unscrupulous attorneys that we are coming after you. And that we will use the U.S. Justice Department and the U.S. Secret Service Department to dispel, dissipate, disperse these unscrupulous attorneys from America's legal system. That is, if they refuse to repent, turn away from their rotten ways, they will be discovered and dealt with by the majority of decent, respectable society.

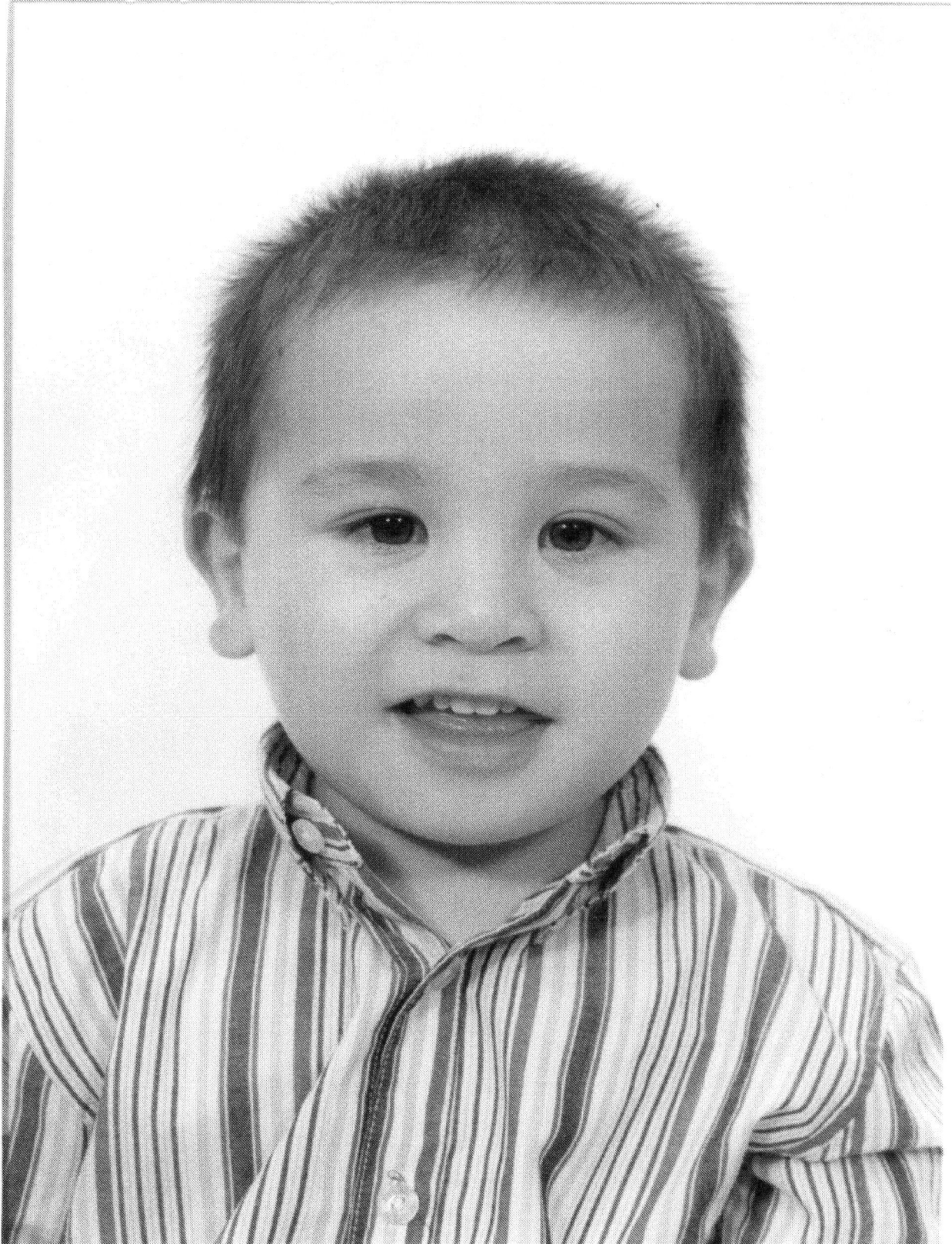

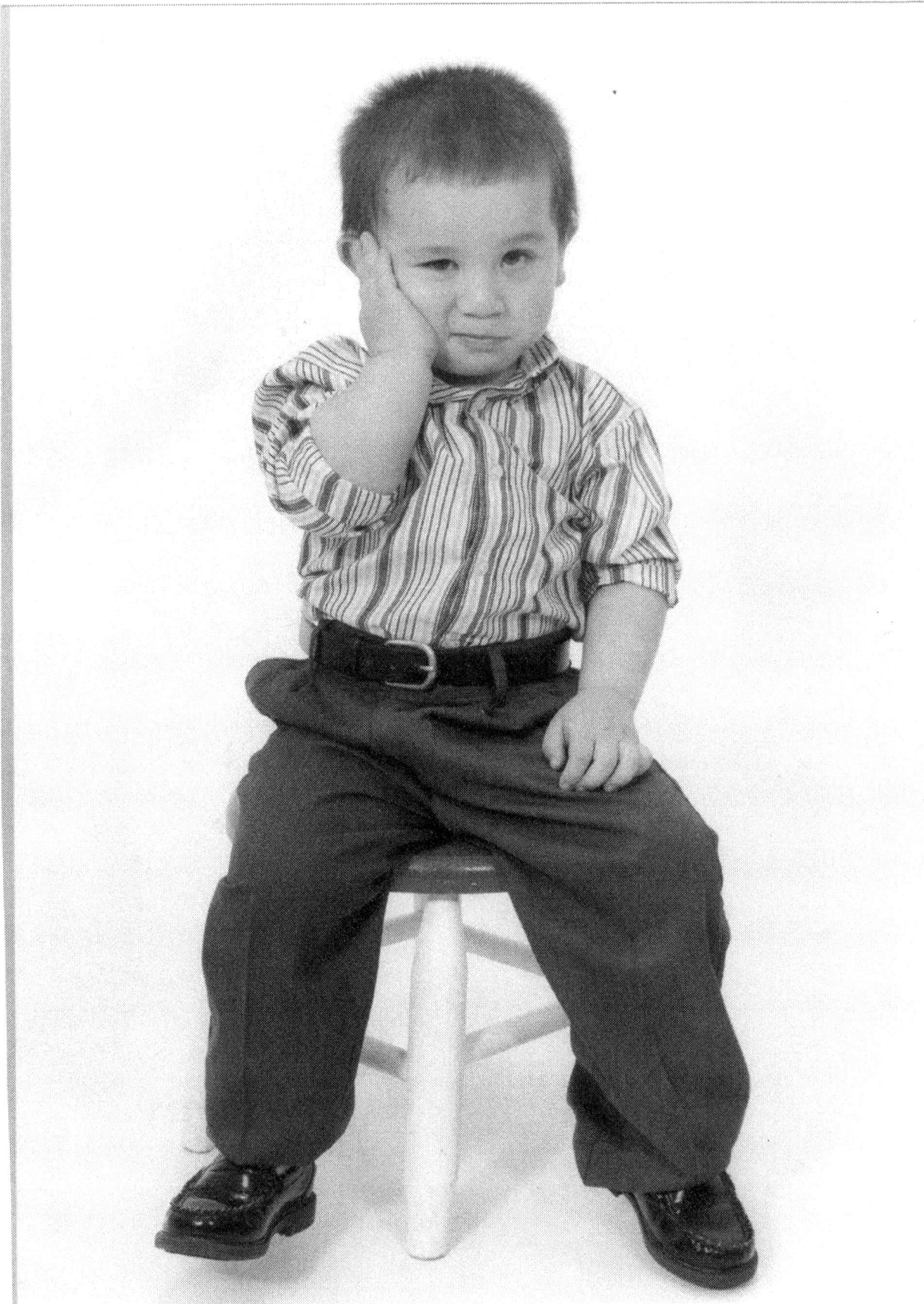

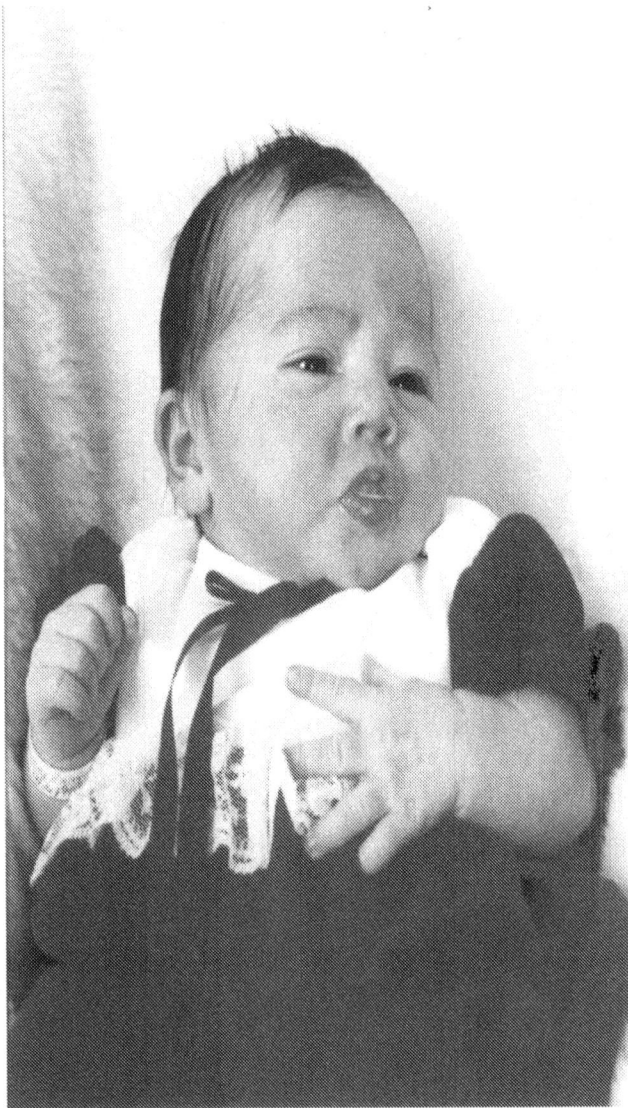
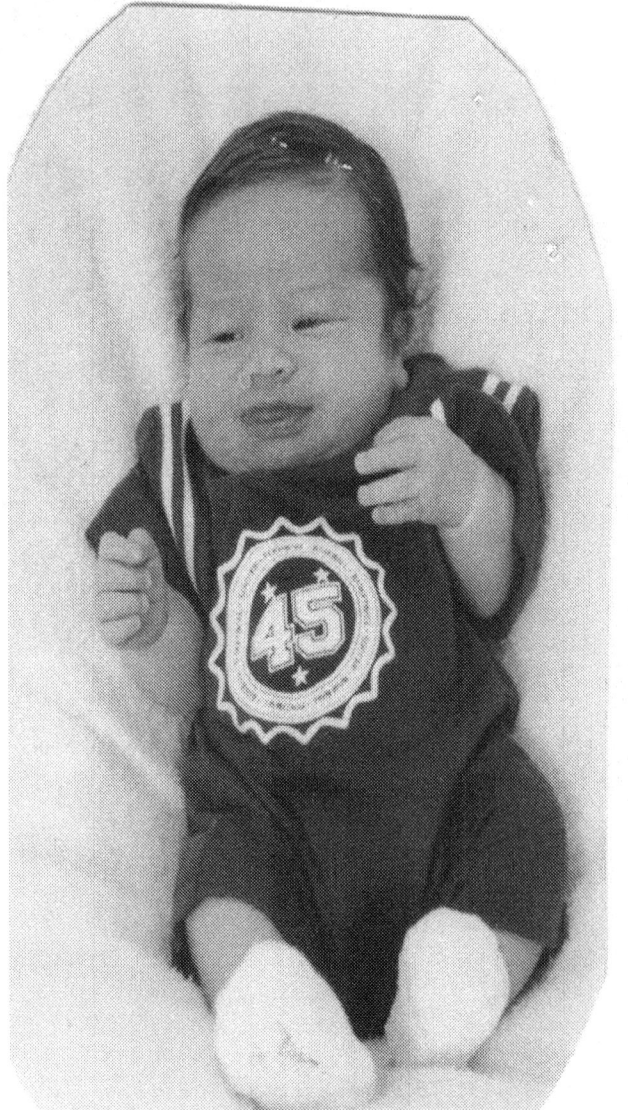

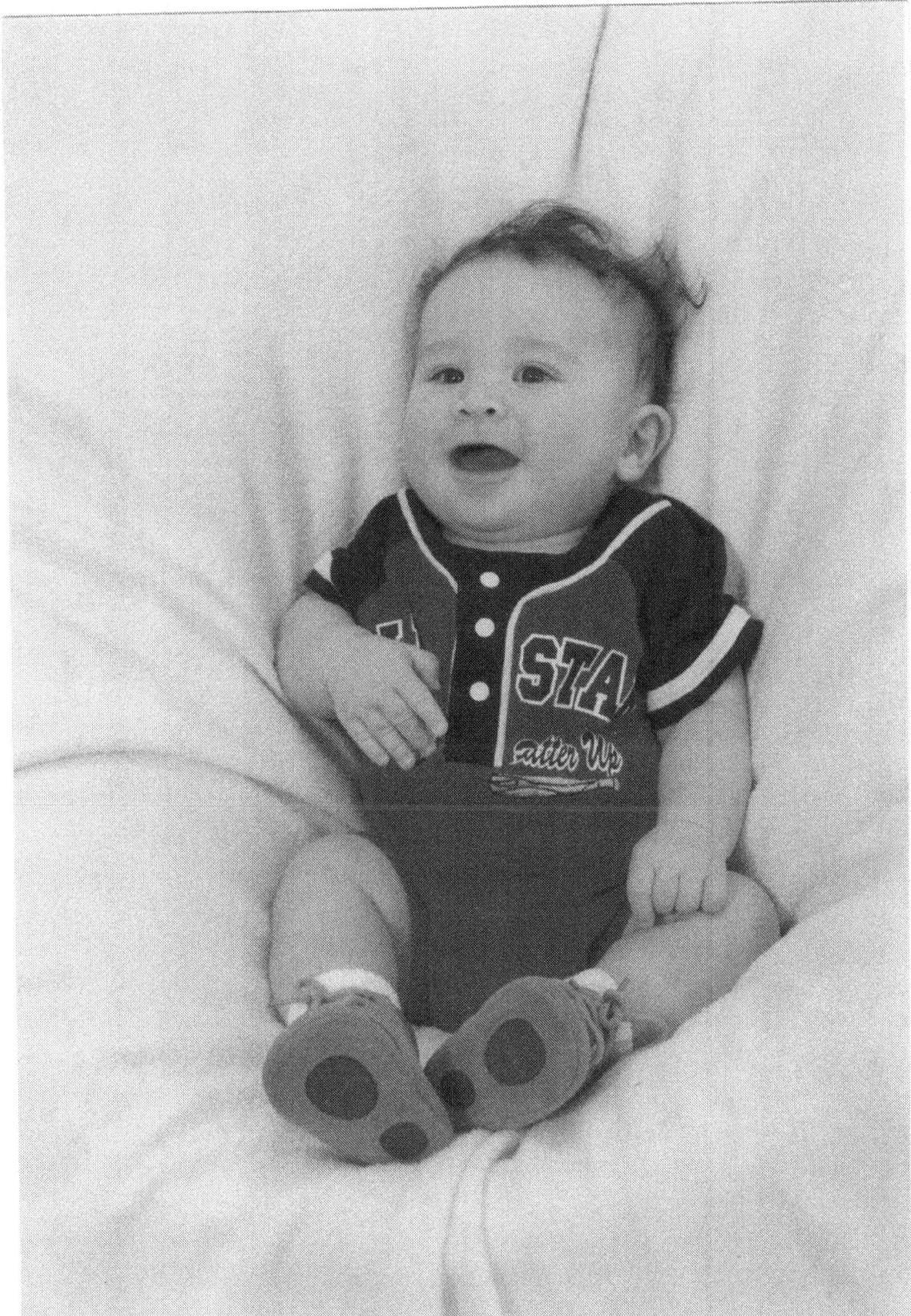

THE RIGHT CHOICE IN LAUNEIL "NEIL" SANDERS WITH HIS 900 MILLION

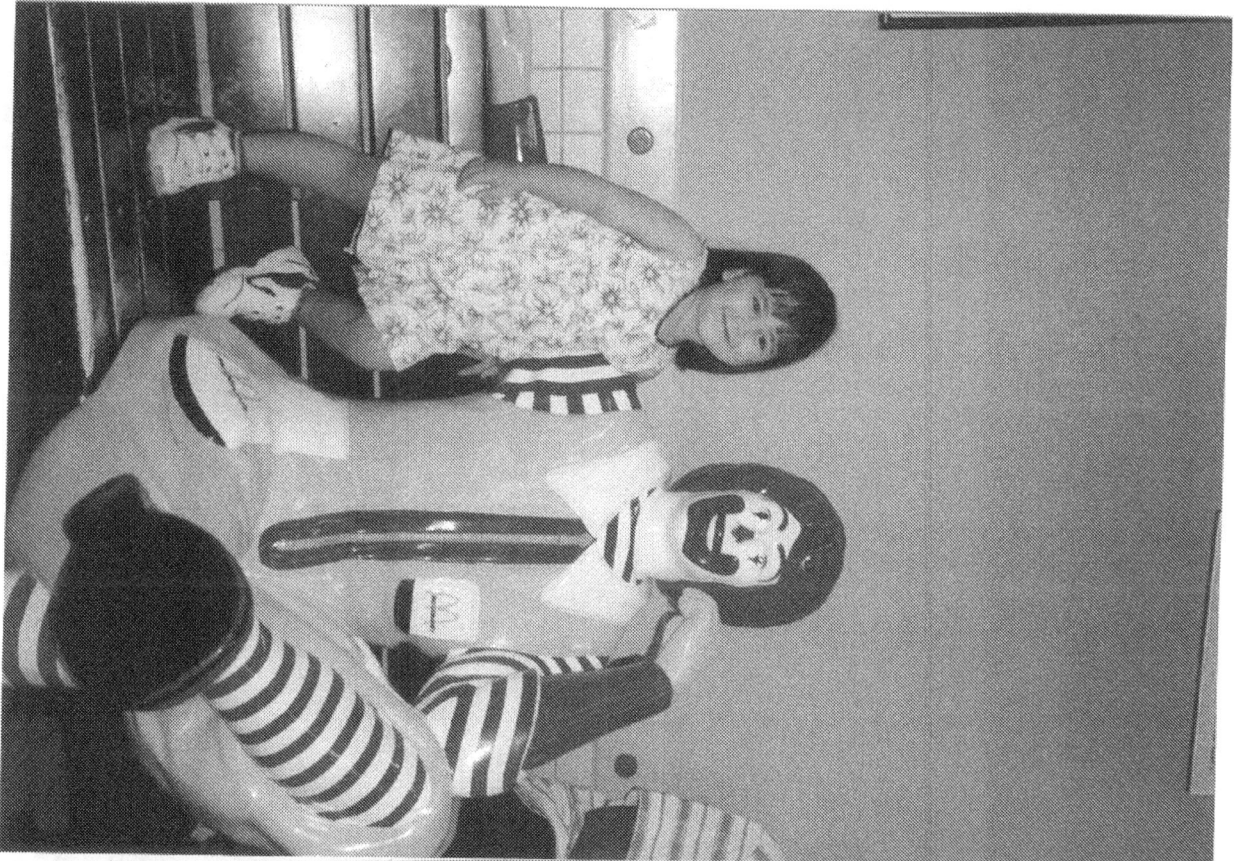

116

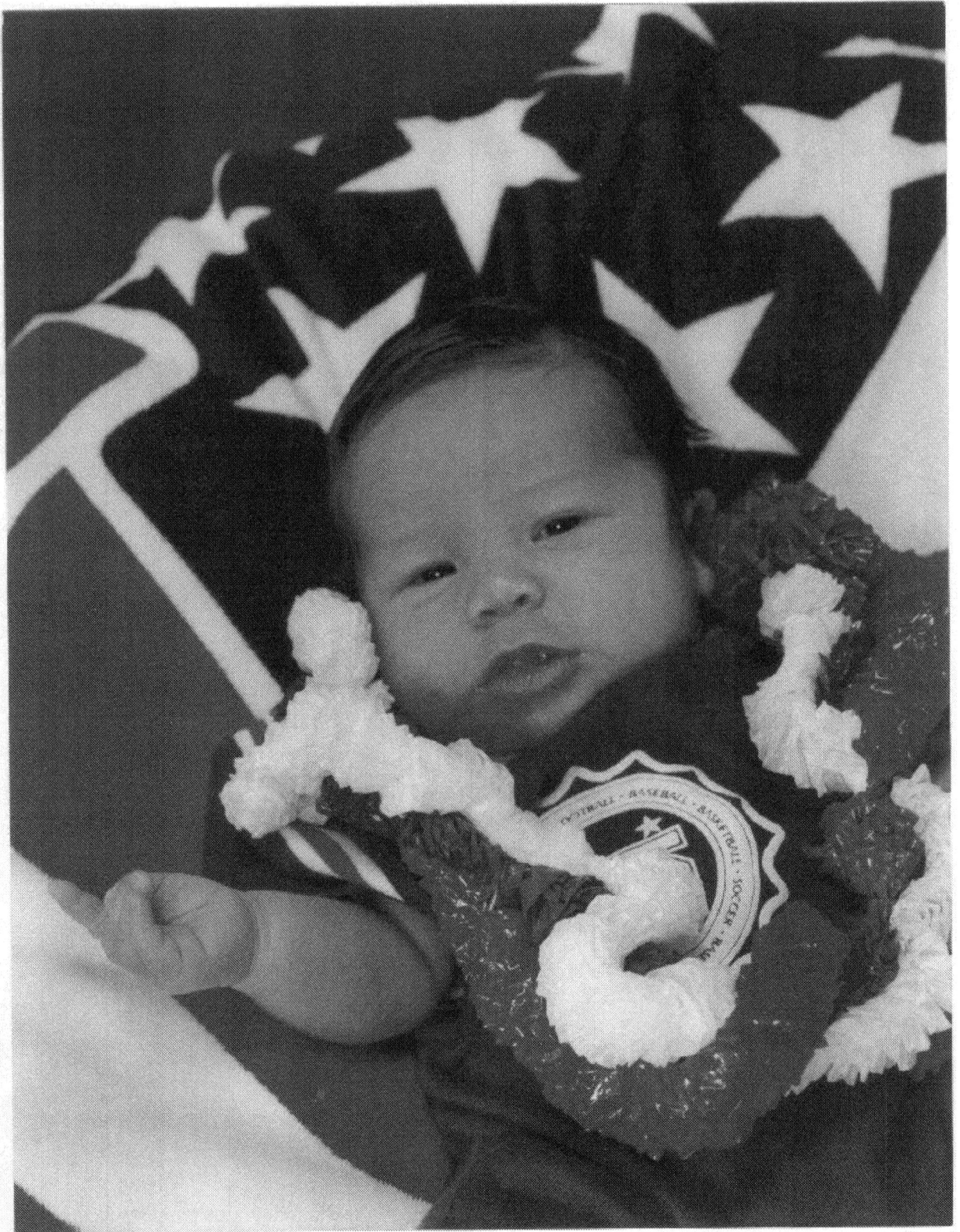

That its 1998 now, and I have spent the past two years in running for Congress as the "only environmental candidate", and in trying to obtain justice and access to America's federal courts. But over these past two years of trying to get access to America's federal courts as a Pro Se litigant, I have discovered it's impossible. It really is "mission impossible". I have to truly tell you that I really believe that America's judicial system is totally broken. President George W. Bush in May 1, 2003 onthe aircraft carrier out from San Diego said "Mission Accomplished" respect to two months' involvement in the Iraq War; and that all combat was over! However, the mission hadn't even begun. Now, July 2006, some 1410 days later, almost four years, there is full civil war in Iraq, over 2650 of our Godly men and women soldiers killed in Iraq (July 2006) and with over 25,000 American men and women soldiers injured for life. Our government has lied to us for the past six years. On my Vietnam War tie shirt it states "All Gave Some and Some Gave All!" Thus, now in April 2007, approximately 3800 American men and women soldiers have given the ultimate: "Their lives for the freedoms, liberties, pursuit of happiness for which our great U.S. Constitution and Declaration of Independence stands for!"

And this was written in July 2006 when we only had these 2600 deaths of American Soldiers in Iraq. Now fast forward to January 2007, where we had the largest number of America soldiers killed in Iraq in one month, over 110 in December 2006! The Vietnam War, where 58,256 Godly men and women soldiers were killed, and also where our government also lied to us for over eighteen years, creates the confirmed judgment that history repeats itself. When I substitute in our Spartanburg County schools system, I ask if they know how many Americans gave their lives in the Vietnam War, and never has any student known the answer. Ken Mehlman, Chairman of the Republican National

Party, on MSNBC's "Hardball with Chris Mathews" and MSNBC's "Keith Olbermann's Countdown" the other evening stated we didn't want to "cut and run from Iraq just as we had done in Vietnam." Well, you stupid, dumb, ignorant, disgraceful, whippersnapper Mehlman, after a government was put into place in 1967, more than 38,000 of those American soldiers were killed until the Vietnam War ended. Thus, after a government was established in South Vietnam, "sound familiar to Iraq." So thus, Mehlman, if we stay in Iraq as long as we were in Vietnam, do you think we will have 75,000 or 150,000 Americans killed? But, I would like to think that it would not take Americans as long as it took during the Vietnam War.

Again, Mr. Mehlman, those 58,256 did not die in vain, "they gave all Honorably for this Great Country just as the 3,800 whom have given all in this Political Iraq war! Americans did, I believe, reflected their total malcontent with the Iraq War at the ballot box. There are a lot of similarities with Vietnam and Iraq. Did we learn anything? I worship the "Prince of Peace." We should be sending missionaries and having more open discussions with everyone in the Middle East. We were told a lot of lies so that Cheney, Rumsfeld, and rest of the hawks could claim and justify the Iraq War by the fraudulent falsehood that Iraq had weapons of mass destruction. You know, Secretary of Defense Rumsfeld should have been fired in 2003. Now this was written in July 2006 before the November 7, 2006, National Election; and, of course, Bush said Rumsfeld was going to be in his office for all the remaining two years of his second term. (However, on November 8, 2008, Bush decided since the Great Citizens the Great United States of America had spoken on November 7, 2006, Rumsfeld had to go early!) However, prior we have criminal dereliction of the

Secretary's duties and responsibilities as he sent our troops into combat without proper body Armour, without the military vehicles being equipped with body Armour; and secondly, the abandonment of the Iraqi army by Rumsfeld and Bremmer was criminal negligence in April 2003. This demanded Rumsfeld's immediate firing. And now we are here in August 2006, and we have had at least ten retired generals and other high ranking officers call for Rumsfeld's firing; however he has not been fired! So, who is the President? Is it this infected Cheney who met secretly with all the energy, oil conglomerates (included Ken Lay who died this week, and the Enron Chairman & CEO Ken Lay with Enron accomplice Jeffrey Skilling who ripped off the state of California and its citizens for 41 billion dollars of electricity. They also ripped off all the investors and employees for billions of dollars back in 2001 and 2002) Cheney promised $3.00 to $4.00 per gallon gasoline and $100.00 per barrel oil pricing. Or is it Bush? From all the exact happenings in the past six years, it certainly is evident that Cheney along with Karl Rove have been the President. And just this first quarter of 2006 it was Cheney who shot in the face one of his Republican comrades at a Texas bird hunt. Low and behold, all of these Cheney and Bush administration believe they are above the law. And even though Cheney shot his fellow associate in the face with his shotgun, he didn't have to give a breath analyzer test to any local or state governmental police agency. That violation, fringe of our judicial system would not be afforded to the rest of America's citizens. The philosophy is that Cheney, Rumsfeld, Bush and the rest of this administration are above the rule of law.

I filed a Whistleblower Environmental Clean Air Act suit in April 14,

1997, Case No 6: 97-998-20AK against Engelhard Corporation and its Corporate Officers when I announced that I was running for the U.S. 4th Congressional seat of South Carolina as the "only environmental candidate." I knew I could make a difference in 1998, and even though I was unsuccessful then, I still know I can make a difference in the Godly lives of men, women, and children of America. I have been standing in the gap for Jesus Christ and for South Carolina's and our nation's environment for the past seventeen years. I have seen that most politicians that I have campaigned against or those in Washington don't really care about the environment.

U. S. FEDERAL ENVIRONMENTAL WHISTLEBLOWER SUIT AGAINST ENGELHARD CORPORATION AND U.S EPA ADMINISTRATOR, CAROL BROWNER

After my conversation with Sue Jones, I learned that Engelhard's nearest neighbor, Cecil Cox had died. Virgil Burkett also had died. I was depressed. I decided to file this federal environmental lawsuit and see if I could help these citizens around Engelhard.

But the suit was dismissed on technicality without any witnesses, testimony, or evidence ever being presented. Pro Se litigants' suits are corruptly, illegally dismissed on technicalities! Now after years in the federal district court in Greenville Division and the appeal to the 4th Federal Circuit Appeals Court in Richmond, Virginia, the U.S. Supreme Court refused to accept my Writ of Certiorari # 97-2629 from the U.S. 4th Circuit Appeals Court. You see, the U.S. Supreme Court would not hear my Writ # 97-2629 (with no witnesses, no testimony, no evidence and no hearings ever held. U.S. District Judge Henry Herlong would not appoint counsel for me.) But Engelhard Corporation has flagrantly, recklessly violated the Clean Air Act for the past 18 years and owes the U.S Treasury approximately 175 million dollars in air permit violations. There is no variance

125

for criminally felony murdering citizens and flagrantly criminally covering up your violations. They emitted thousands of tons of toxic, hazardous air pollutants in violation of their permit. Access to the U.S. Federal Courts was never allowed. U.S. Federal Judge Herlong spent $1,700,000 for imported Honduran paneling, decorations, but would not let the Greenville News or any other South Carolina citizen tour his newly renovated U.S. Federal Chambers! The Greenville News published in their newspaper in September 6, 1998, that Judge Henry Herlong had directly abused his office, had spent a $1,500,000 of Honduran imported paneling to modernize his chambers with tax dollars. However he refused to let any South Carolina citizens into his chambers to view his newly $1,700,000 modernized taxpayers' chambers. There are laws on the books, that any more than $1,500,000 spent on U.S. Courthouse improvements, requires Congress to approve it! However, the Greenville Division Haynesworth U.S. Federal Courthouse spent $4,500,000 on the polluted, tainted, contaminated, defiled, wicked, decayed, putrid, infected, rotten federal courthouse.

The Clean Air Act does allow Citizens Suits similar to mine. However, they have to have an attorney and then maybe you get access. I really believe Congress (in 1999 Congressman Henry Hyde, Chairman of House U.S. Judiciary Committee around this time and Senator Orrin Hatch, Chairman of Senate U.S. Judiciary at this time in 1999) should have passed new laws. There should be a U.S. Federal law that prohibits U.S. Magistrates and U.S. District Judges from dismissing for any reasons any U.S. Federal Lawsuits filed by Pro Se litigants. And furthermore, laws would be revised. The new law should state that a U.S. Magistrates or U.S. District Judges must appoint counsel for Pro Se litigants {mandatory for all cases}. And that Rules 6 and 12 of the Federal Rules of

Civil Procedures of 28 USCA Annotated would be repealed, and that Summary Judgments are repealed and eliminated. The system must be revamped in order that Pro Se litigant cases have to go to jury trial for determination of their cases. Summary Judgment is eliminated and these criminal dirty tricks would no longer be law. All Pro Se litigants will, by revised U.S. Federal law, have counsel appointed, and obtain mandatory trial to try to prove their case in federal court. Just as the Honorable U.S. Supreme Court ruled in Polk Company v. Glover, the Court ruled that the plaintiffs had made out a Premia Facie case, reversed and remanded back to District Court for taking of evidence, witnesses and testimony.

My immediate supervisor at Engelhard was Rodney Kutz, environmental engineer, at their Seneca, South Carolina, plant. They produced specialty precious metals of Platinum, Palladium, Silver, Gold, and Rhodium. As mentioned earlier, there were no accurate emissions calculations in 1988. Engelhard Corporation really didn't know what their Potential To Emit (PTE) without control equipment emissions were! Nor did they know what their actual emissions, Allowable Emissions (Allowable Emissions After Control Equipment) were. Rodney Kutz, had performed a few of the engineering calculations, and my contract position was to perform all the remaining emissions calculations to assist in preparation of the said Title V, Part 70 Clean Air Act Permit Submittal to SCDHEC.

Engelhard hired a Clemson chemical engineer in the summer of 1994, but his performance was unsatisfactory. So I got a chance for the position. Since the submittal of Title V, Part 70 Air Permit was postponed until Spring 1996, my contract was extended until my last day on September 23, 1996. The last half of 1996 I worked only part-time at approximately 24 hours per week. One of the most revealing facts was that when you reviewed the Operating Permit from SCDHEC for the three Tri –Mer ™ wet scrubbers; you discovered how many excess tons of toxic, hazardous air pollutants that Engelhard had been actually emitting. For when you compared the permitted emissions and what they were actually emitting, it was clear why all vegetation including trees around the plant surroundings were dead. And it was no coincidence that Sue Jones, her husband Don Jones, and other neighbors surrounding said Engelhard were contacting various severe respiratory diseases! Engelhard was emitting huge excesses of tons of nitrogen oxides {both nitrous oxides and nitrogen dioxides} from their Tri –Mer™ Scrubber ID # 21-01, which was designated as their NOx Scrubber 21-01 {both nitrous oxides and nitrogen dioxides}. In addition in this same scrubber 21-01, said Engelhard was emitting huge tons of Hydrogen Chloride gases and Hydrochloric Acid mist.

A second Tri –Mer ™ wet scrubber was named the No-NOx scrubber, scrubber ID # 21-02. This scrubber was called the No-NOx as all vents from reactions that vented to ID 21-02 were supposed to contain no oxides of nitrogen. However, huge quantities, large tonnage per year of Hydrogen Chloride gases in excess of their permitted limits were emitted from this emission source stack 21-02.

The third Tri –Mer ™ scrubber was the Ammonia Scrubber, stack ID # 21-03. This wet scrubber was in severe, dilapidated, deteriorated shape. I mentioned before that this was a piece of junk scrubber purchased on the cheap. There had not been any thorough engineering evaluation by a professional environmental engineer, who could have specified the proper design! This scrubber did emit certain quantities of ammonia at various times. When the jury-rigged sulfuric acid pump stopped, the pH of the scrubber liquid was elevated way above a pH of 8.33, emitting hundreds of thousands of tons of ammonia. Above a pH of 8.33, the ammonia gases were emitted in a large ammonia plume cloud.

In 1994 because of several nitrogen dioxides emissions test performed on the Oxides of Nitrogen Scrubber, Stack ID 21-01, Engelhard Corporation entered into a Consent Order with SCDHEC to install a new Ceilcote™ wet scrubber for replacement of 21-01 scrubber. The Consent Order stated a Compliance Operation date by June 1, 1995. Thus, this construction of this new Ceilcote™ scrubber was initiated just prior to my contract initiation and prior to my contract in October 1994. However, in January 1995, I mentioned to Rod Kutz about installing a Continuous EPA Certified Continuous Emission Monitor (CEM); however Rod Kutz's answer to me was infamous.

Congress wrote into the Enforcement Provisions of said Clean Air Act that there are $1,000,000 penalties for criminal violations. Additionally, Congress wrote into the Clean Air Act Amendments of 1977 that there were mandatory "Non Compliance Penalties for Industries Who failed to Install Proper Air Pollution Control Equipment," and that there were "Triple Damages for Cost of Avoided Air Pollution and Economic Benefit to industry." Thus, if the cost of three new scrubbers for Engelhard Corporation were $10,500,000; then the treble damages that EPA Administrator could access Engelhard would have been approximately $31,500.000!

Engelhard had posted on company bulletin boards that former employee, Paul Fryer, who had been terminated, was trying to contact current employees. The notice said, "If Paul Fryer tried to contact current existing employees, that the current

129

employees were to offer no information and were to notify Engelhard's Corporate legal department in Iselin, New Jersey." I noted Paul Fryer's name and after my contract ended in September 23, 1996, I phoned Paul Fryer and met with him twice after finishing my contract. I had asked Bill Griffin about Paul Fryer, the former employee. Bill Griffin said he was suing under Age Discrimination Laws. Since he, Fryer, was suing, "his lawsuit" probably kept Rod Kutz from firing him, Bill Griffin. Thus, because of Paul Fryer's suit, Griffin was transferred out of the Utilities to a new area away from Rod Kutz. But he was allowed to keep his job. I know Rodney Kutz gave a deposition in Paul Fryer's suit as he reviewed his deposition prior with Engelhard's attorneys one Sunday night prior to his Monday morning deposition. One of the items I would not find out until I met with Paul Fryer was that Engelhard Corporation doctors had diagnosed Paul Fryer with "Platinosis Disease." Paul later told me he had all the symptoms, and that was why Engelhard had decided to terminate him.

Shortly after my contract was finished at Engelhard, I received a call at my Spartanburg home from a SCDHEC criminal investigator, Paul Cavanaugh. Mr. Cavanaugh came to my Spartanburg home one morning around October 3, 1996. He said he had an on-going criminal investigation of Engelhard Corporation in Seneca, South Carolina. Current insider Engelhard Employees gave my name to SCDHEC, I supposed. They gave SCDHEC my correct address and my correct Spartanburg telephone number. I assumed current Engelhard employees gave it to Cavanaugh.{they knew they would be fired if their identities were revealed.) I agreed to meet in Columbia, South Carolina, at SCDHEC headquarters on 2nd floor of 2600 Bull Street, Columbia, South Carolina. I did meet with Mr. Cavanaugh and other SCDHEC employees on at least two other occasions at SCDHEC's offices at 2600 Bull Street, Columbia, South Carolina. I thought that Mr. Cavanaugh would eventually get a criminal search warrant and criminally search said Engelhard's premises for other evidence of their criminal racketeering and criminal felony violations of Clean Air Act. However, this never occurred. I can only speculate why no criminal search warrants were ever issued. But in South Carolina for a very long time the SCDHEC has had a very cozy relationship with industries. Anything you wanted, you got it. The late Roy Orbison recorded a great song "Anything you want, You Got It!" And this was SCDHEC's relationship with industry. I was very disappointed by the facts that Paul Cavanaugh and the SCDHEC agency, that was supposed to be protecting South Carolina's citizens from health hazards and imminent death from industries, failed! SCDHEC has not been enforcing our State's Environmental Pollution Laws and our Federal Environmental Laws (in this case, the Clean Air Act)

Thus, in April 1997 (right after the Spartanburg Herald-Journal announced and published in April 12, 1997, that I was seeking the U.S. 4th Congressional seat as the as Republican Ultraconservative "Only Environmental Candidate"), I brought suit in U.S. Federal District Court. I paid my $150.00 in U.S. Federal Court, Greenville Division, on April 14, 1997, as mentioned earlier. I really felt that since I would be filing affidavits before the Federal District Court, this time, I would get to go to trial with discovery, witnesses, depositions, cross-exams and subpoenas. However, I was wrong again. U.S. District Judge Henry Herlong was not interested in righteousness and justice. As the waitress at the Spartanburg Veterans of Foreign Wars Club stated after she read Judge Herlong's November 17, 1997, dismissal "it seemed totally unfair." She asked "if I was going to appeal Herlong's decision?" I told her, yes! Of course, it was useless. I eventually filed Writ of Certiorari with U.S. Supreme Court also, and they didn't care about justice either or the hundreds of thousands dying! As one of my goals in writing my biography is getting reforms, and that all Pro Se litigants' suits must be allowed a jury trial as our Constitution states.

1. That I want to give testimony and witness to Congress in for them to repeal 28 USCA Rules 6 and Rule 12, and to write into law that all Pro Se litigants and all plaintiffs shall and must be given trial by JURY.

2. That I want to give more authority to Citizens Suits under our U.S. Federal Environmental Laws, and make it mandatory under these new tort reform laws that all plaintiffs get a jury trial.

3. That I want to make it mandatory that a U.S. Federal District Judge has to conduct Preliminary Injunction testimony, witnesses hearing, and make ruling on Preliminary Injunction concerning all and any of our U.S. Federal Environmental Laws. That no U.S. Magistrates may enter on any matters in U.S. Federal Environmental Laws. And that no Magistrates shall be able to dismiss citizens, Pro Se suits. Rather Congress would better serve the citizens of this great country if all U.S. Magistrates were fired. We should not have to wait until hundreds of thousands or more citizens have died of respiratory cancers before anyone does something! Congress needs to be made aware that the U.S. Federal District and especially the U.S. 4th Circuit Appellate Court in Richmond, Virginia, are not upholding the laws passed by Congress. They are not upholding their U.S. Federal Oaths to uphold the U.S. Federal Environmental Laws passed by Congress!

4. That Congress should have mandatory provisions to immediately hear Environmental Complaints by any of its citizens on violations of any environmental laws.

And these immediate hearings would be before the Senate Environmental & Public Works Committee and the House Environment and Public Works Committee. And that Congress have signed into Law that these Committees have authority, power and prestige and funds available for immediate appointment of counsel (s) for any Pro Se and or Environmental Groups appearing before them. This will give Congress more added assurances that the U. S. Federal Courts cannot thumb their fingers or spit in the face of Congress in defiance of our Congress. (There is plenty of Judicial Activism at present in our federal courts.)

5.   That Congress should have mandatory provisions to immediately require by New Law that all U.S. District Courts and all U.S. Circuit Appeals Courts {all TEN Federal Circuits} report semi- annually with status reports of all lawsuits of Environmental Laws. And that these Committees may recommend disciplinary action to the Judiciary Committees of any misconduct by a U.S. District Judge and or U.S. Circuit Appeals Judge.

Having complied with the 60 days notice of CAA (Clean Air Act), I filed suit on Monday April 14, 1997. I really was discouraged in the fact that Paul Cavanaugh and our own SCDHEC were not going to do anything to protect South Carolina's Great Citizens from death by flagrant, criminal violations of Clean Air Act by Engelhard. Why do you think that in all of these U.S. Federal District Courts when a Pro Se litigant files a suit, the Court is prejudiced and dismisses on technicalities with no witnesses, evidence or testimony allowed! These U. S. Federal Judges make $190,000 in salary annually, but normal citizens cannot get access. The Constitution, established by our Forefathers some 230 years ago, clearly states all should have access to the Courts. I do believe some of all our Forefathers who established our Constitution some 230 years ago, would vomit all over some of our federal judges and lawyers.

I believe God's plan will turn around America. I pray that more Christians will get involved in our political process. Maybe a National Revival {see the organization of two and one half million government disciples in Chapter 18} will get us started on that correct path. In 1999 I commuted 190 miles a day from Spartanburg, South Carolina to Columbia, South Carolina, and return. I accepted the Associate Environmental Engineer position with SCDHEC in Bureau of Water, Domestic Wastewater Permitting. (It is now August 1999) On my trip down in the morning and back to Spartanburg in the evening for the three hours commuting I listened to Evangelist Billy Graham's Blue Ridge Broadcasting station WMIT-FM, 106.9 out of Black Mountain, North Carolina. Everyday, I listen to Pastor Greg Laurie, of "Harvest Crusades, A New Beginning". I really love to hear Pastor Greg Laurie preach. I wish that I were as advanced spiritually as Pastor Greg Laurie. He had a Harvest crusade from the First Union Spectrum in the weekend of August 20, 1999, through Sunday August 22, 1999. The past few days he has been preaching from Revelations, Chapter 2, which has really been inspiring. His sermon yesterday was "On Compromise." One of the original seven churches of the Lord compromised everything! Pastor Greg Laurie mentioned the Christian Student at Columbine High School who was in the media, Cathy Bernol. As when the killers Harris and Klebold asked her if she was a Christian, she did not waiver. She did not compromise and stated to the two evil killers of the devil "I do accept Jesus Christ as my personal savior and am a Christian!" And, of course, we know, Harris and Klebold shot her and murdered her for her beliefs, her faith, and trust in the Lord and our Savior. Pastor Greg

Laurie pointed out Cathy Bernol's supreme sacrifice and supreme persecution. As he said just as Cathy did, we all should strive in walking with our Lord! Truly, Cathy Bernol was "whisked away in the twinkle of an eye" to be with our Lord Jesus Christ in the micro, micro second he was describing. That's how we will experience in the second coming of Jesus Christ. If some of the unscrupulous attorneys in America had the supreme sacrifice that Cathy Bernol demonstrated, we would have a more civil decent society here in this earthly world. I know as what Pastor Ed Deese preached one Sunday from Romans and said "We, as Christians and believers, have to sacrifice our bodies in the life of Jesus Christ." Cathy Bernol achieved that witnessing for Jesus Christ, Our Father's Holy Word stresses that in the Chapter of Romans. She sacrificed her life in the body of Christ.

11

MY CANDIDACY FOR U.S. CONGRESS, U.S. 4TH DISTRICT OF SOUTH CAROLINA, {UPSTATE PIEDMONT, GREENVILLE, SPARTANBURG, UNION COUNTY and PART OF LAURENS COUNTY}

That around April 1, 1997, Sue Jones, a neighbor of Engelhard Corporation in Seneca, South Carolina, called me and told me that Engelhard's nearest neighbor Cecil Cox died on March 25, 1997. She had spent several hours talking with him on several occasions, "and she said he said he had been continually harassed by Engelhard." And those kinds of tactics do not surprise me one bit as one Seneca doctor who testified against Engelhard in the 1987 Permit Approval Process was also harassed by said Engelhard. His medical practice in the Seneca area was destroyed. Since Virgil Burkett had died some six months earlier and now Cecil Cox, Engelhard's nearest neighbor now had died, I decided that I would run for the open U.S. Congressional Seat (said above U. S. 4th District South Carolina) that Congressman Bob Inglis was vacating voluntarily to make a run for U.S. Senator, seat of Ernest Hollings. Thus, I talked with the Spartanburg Herald-Journal, and on Saturday, April 12, 1997, the <u>Herald-Journal</u> ran the short article detailing why I was running as "the only Environmental Candidate." The widow of Cecil Cox was very scared of Engelhard. She had witnessed the continued harassment of her husband by said Engelhard. I decided to stand firm and file this lawsuit, as I knew the corrupt agents W. Thomas Lavender and Paul Cavanaugh of SCDHEC were not going to do anything. Therefore I would file this federal lawsuit and force EPA to enforce the Clean Air Act and force implementation of the Clean Air Act as had been authorized by Congress. However, I would soon learn the U.S. Federal Judicial System is not about search for truth and justice and the performing of trials, but corruptly denies access to Pro Se litigants! It is simply about playing the corrupt Satan's agents dirty lawyer tricks and games.

Engelhard had burned unauthorized, unallocated, non-permitted wastes resulting in tons of illegal emissions to neighbors and citizens in the surrounding area. Someone had to step-up to the plate, and I, Colonel Launeil "Neil" Sanders was that concerned environmentalist and a two decades experienced environmental engineer citizen who would take on those responsibilities. However, I was later to learn even more about America's Federal Judicial System. This would plunge me deeper into disparity. "You can't ever get equitable access and any judicial relief if you are a Pro Se Litigant in America's corrupt federal courts."

I knew that SCDHEC and EPA were not performing their duties and responsibilities in protecting South Carolina's citizens from imminent threat of death. A great deal of friends and citizens I have met and talked with in South Carolina knew that SCDHEC was not performing their duties under the law. Just as Honorable Dever

Melton, a resident next to the now closed down Laidlaw Hazardous Wastes Incinerator in Roebuck, South Carolina, where there have been documented over 300 respiratory cancer cases with approximately 129 deaths, said "the SCDHEC is corrupt, and they don't really care about misconduct and the pollution of Industry! It's all about how much clout, authority and money, the industries, have!"

Before I filed this suit I knew that Citizens Suits were allowed by Clean Air Act passed by Congress; and that you had to notify EPA Administrator 60 days notice that you as citizen plan to bring suit in Federal Court. Thus, I originally sent EPA Administrator in November 3, 1996, the original 60 days Notice of Intent to Sue Under Citizens Provisions of Clean Air Act. Then, in November 19, 1996, I had an appointment and went to see the most experienced Environmental Attorney in Spartanburg, Mr. Gary Poliakoff. Gary Poliakoff said I should revise the 60 Days Notice to EPA Administrator Carol Browner. In January 1997, I did revise the 60 days Notice to EPA Administrator. Mr. Poliakoff said he would not represent me unless I got some of Engelhard employees to come forward and testify and act as plaintiffs in suit. However, I knew this was not going to be impossible as no current employees were going to come forward as they knew they would be immediately fired (just as Paul Fryer was fired!). Secondly, Paul Cavanaugh of SCDHEC had information and evidence from other sources on Engelhard's criminal racketeering, criminal violations of Clean Air Act. As you will see I have filed many notarized affidavits before U.S. Magistrate Catoe and U.S. District Judge Henry Herlong. However because Magistrate Catoe and Herlong hate all Pro Se litigants, you can never obtain access. It really makes you sick to your guts that you know the system is so corrupt no matter whether you are in Family Law State Court, U.S. Federal

District Court, and the U.S. 4th Circuit Federal Appeals Court in Richmond.

A new law that would eventually give everyone fair and equal access in bringing forth witnesses, testimony, evidence, at trial before juries in trying to prove their cases is mandatory. Real Tort Reform is mandatory, and Congress must pass new regulations. All Pro Se and Citizens suits as described in earlier chapters should be implemented and allowed jury trials.

That all cases filed have to be allowed to go to trial as stated above, and a *New U.S. New Fees and Compensation Schedule* would be signed into law and it would consist of minimum:

a.   List

(1)   That in all cases the following would apply:

That whatever the total amount of the award by the jury or presiding Judge at Trial (as now there is no Summary Judgment, as it is repealed) would be allocated as follows {And any Punitive awards would have a Maximum Punitive CAPS of 9:1 of the said Compensatory Awards and would be allocated in said same allocation percentages}

PARTY	PERCENT ALLOCATION OF AWARD
Plaintiff (s)	40
Defendant(s)	Allow a credit of 15
Plaintiff (s)' Counsels	20
Defendant (s)' Counsels	15
U.S. Federal Court Fees	10

($150.00 filing fees eliminated; and resultant filing appeal fees to U.S. Circuit Courts and U.S. Supreme Courts are eliminated)

This New U.S. Federal Law would encourage settlement of more lawsuits, would guarantee Pro Se litigants fair and equal access, and would guarantee more justice and equitable treatment for all plaintiffs and defendants. And it would provide attorney fees to both the plaintiffs and defendant attorneys, no matter who is winning party in cases where damages are awarded. This Fair Equitable Allocation of Monetary Awards will serve our citizens best in restoring Justice and Truth and Righteousness to the U.S. Federal Justice System; and additionally would make it mandatory for trials of all suits as the corrupt, corrupt dismissals like Summary Judgment and other corrupt dismissals via Rules 6 and 12 are eliminated. Thus, all parties' counsels will get an equitable percentage.

And today, since I am a Shareholder of CBS television stock I received today copies of proposed settlement of shareholders suit {8 ½ year old suit in U.S. Federal District Court of Western Pennsylvania} by our plaintiffs attorneys for settlement of the case for $67,250,000. This is prime example of what I'm talking about, as this case has been dismissed on technicalities without any evidence, witnesses, trial etc.; three times dismissed by U.S. District Judges. All the horse manure, all the bull has to stop as you see even in my environmental case where hundreds have died, because of clear civil racketeering and criminal racketeering of Clean Air Act it was dismissed by triple corrupt lawyer playing games. Congress must change this! Certainly, our CBS plaintiffs' lawyers in Paoli, Pennsylvania, and Haverford, Pennsylvania, have to be commended, complimented on their perseverance in not quitting before CBS finally decided to address the misconduct of previous officers of previous Westinghouse prior to becoming CBS Inc.

The SCDHEC system is filled with polluted, depraved, tainted, defiled, vitiated, wicked, decayed, putrid, infected and rotten racketeering based on giving industry anything they want. Like W. Thomas Lavender, whose relative worked for Engelhard Corporation; Engelhard got any favors they wanted no matter how many South Carolinians were criminally felony murdered! You see, Thomas Lavender had been an attorney at South Carolina Department of Health and Environmental Control. Now he is an attorney in practice with Nexson, Pruitt, Jacobs and Pollard LLC. Cecil Cox, Virgil Burkett and many thousands have died! Paul Fryer was diagnosed with Platinosis Disease, and Engelhard was also being allowed also to emit toxic precious Platinum metals' emissions. Those emissions eventually will terminally kill many former and current employees of said Engelhard. Never can Pro Se litigants conduct evidence, testimony, witnesses, depositions, or any hearings in U.S. Federal District Courts. I am really disappointed in America's Federal Judicial System, as maybe it will take some of our Congressmen and Congresswomen and Senators loved ones to die before there will be changes and retrofit of our Federal Judicial System. Maybe it will take some of the nine U.S. Supreme Court justices' loved ones to die of the corporate polluters for any of us to get access!

I Joined the Spartanburg First Monday Club in June 1997 which met for lunch at the 'First Monday Club', the first Monday of the month, at Wade's Restaurant, Spartanburg, South Carolina. After meeting with Mary Ann Riley, Chairman of Spartanburg County Republicans Women Organization, I paid my dues and joined the said First Monday Club of Spartanburg. I had lunch with Jim Johnson, Chairman of Spartanburg County Republican Party in April 1997, and he told me "he supported Jim DeMint, and that I didn't have a chance and was wasting my time!" From this point, Jim Johnson was not a fair, equitable minded person and it was useless to ask him to help me.

The first meeting, gathering was the August 23, 1997, debate at Wofford College. Dorothy Love and I went to Wofford College that evening. However, Walter McSherry told me at the meeting that Jim Johnson had not allowed me to speak because I had not paid my $2750.00 to the Republican Party in Columbia for the filing fees. I would later learn that these $2750.00 fees to the state party didn't actually have to be paid until March 15, 1998 through March 30, 1998 of the election year. Thus, Jim Johnson is just an outright, pompous, bias, liar who just didn't want me to have an invitation. Walter McSherry acknowledged that I was present at the meeting before the debate. The five candidates at the debate table were Mike Fair, Jim DeMint, Jim Ritchie, Howell Clyborne, and Frank Raddish.

In October 26, 1997, the North Spartanburg Rotary Club extended an invitation to me as well as the five candidates as who spoke at Wofford in August 1997. Thus, this was, at the North Spartanburg Rotary Club Luncheon, my first chance to speak on my "Environmental Candidacy and my other Platform Issues." At this North Spartanburg Rotary Club luncheon, we had a series of about five questions that we all answered. This included opening and closing statements. Of course, I was the only candidate who had his 2¾ years old daughter, Dorothy Love (Dot Love) Sanders with me sitting at the head table.

First Debate at Greenville Technical College on Veterans Night November 11, 1997

That again we the same six candidates were invited to debate at Greenville Tech on this Veterans Night, November 11, 1997. This was first debate at Greenville Tech and our final, second debate, would be back at Greenville Tech on Monday June 1, 1998, a week before the June 9, 1998 Primary. Prior to the final debate on June 1, 1998, my wife was scheduled for her U.S. Naturalization Ceremony and Oath of Allegiance at the U.S. Haynesworth Federal Courthouse on June 5, 1998; I tried to get the local media to cover her swearing in, but was unsuccessful!

At the debate, I remember making comments thanking our Veterans. I was the only veteran of the six candidates on the stage. Howell Clyborne thanked his father, who was a Veteran and was in attendance at the debate. I remember distinctly one of the questions in which both Jim DeMint and Mike Fair made derogatory comments about that South Carolina Industry was over-burdened, over-pressured with too many costly environmental regulations and rules. They believed some relief from these should be forth coming to make room for more industry. Having knowledge what current Governor David Beasley Republican administration was doing in the environmental areas, and at South Carolina Department of Health and Environmental Control, I felt that DeMint and Fair responses of their comments didn't care at all about the environment. I was offended and ashamed that they felt they needed to "play the games with industries to get the environmental laws done away with or weakened!" I made my points that I was a senior environmental engineer professional with over 25 years experience in both, industry and government including over a year with Environmental Protection Agency (EPA) in Research Triangle Park, North

Carolina. And, of course, I got my points in on my environmental suit in U.S. Federal District Court, Greenville, South Carolina, against Engelhard Corporation and the over 130 cases of respiratory cancer deaths here in South Carolina from Laidlaw's Hazardous Wastes Incinerator, Roebuck, South Carolina. Candidates' Debate at Spartanburg First Monday Club at Wade's Restaurant Monday December 1, 1997

Shown on photograph 43,on preceding pages is photo of Janneth's U.S. Naturalization Ceremony at the U.S. Federal Courthouse in Greenville, South Carolina. In this photo from left, her sister Tonnette Williams, Janneth sitting, Launeil and Dorothy Love.

Shown on photograph 44,on preceding pages is photo of Janneth's U.S. Naturalization Ceremony at the U.S. Federal Courthouse in Greenville, South Carolina. In this Janneth E. Sanders ,newly U.S. Naturalized Citizen sworn in on today, June 5, 1998, holding her U.S. Naturalized Certificate.

Shown on photograph 45,on preceding pages is photo of Janneth's U.S. Naturalization Ceremony at the U.S. Federal Courthouse in Greenville, South Carolina. In this first top photo from left, Janneth, Dorothy Love in middle, and Launeil. In the bottom photo, her sister Tonnette Williams, and Janneth.

Again, it was the debate of us, (the said six candidates) and I again made my environmental points. I also referred to the Wall Street Journal, October 9, 1997 as it referred to the 1.69 Trillion 1998 Budget approved by our Congress. This was more than we had spent in the past 153 years! Isn't that a paradox? Now in 2007, Bush's 2007 budget is 2.9 Trillion dollars, a full 1.3 Trillion dollars more than the year 2000 Budget.

In six years the Cheney-Boy Bush Administration has run our country into the ground where our children and grand children will be paying us off the debt for the next 150 years.

At this debate, since I am the owner and President of a small environmental engineering and services corporation, Launeil International Company Inc., I mentioned my grievances against the government on its treatment of small businesses. The U.S. Internal Revenue Service has continually harassed my small business. And one of the first actions after January 2009 would have Congress in 100 days dissolve the U.S. Internal Revenue Service and sign into law a *New Flat Fair Tax Law*. Thus, I definitely favor a National Sales Tax with complete abandonment of US IRS.

I knew that the present Beasley Administration in South Carolina didn't really care about the environment. I wanted to make my environmental points. Additionally, news release out of the Columbia Republican party left out Frank Raddish and Launeil Neil Sanders. Thus, since Frank and I didn't have as much money or notoriety as the other four, we got eliminated via the South Carolina Republican Party News release. We all, six candidates, had participated in over four debates together. I decided to run as an Environmental Conservative Democrat. It was reported that Bill McCuen, a Greenville Accountant, and Glenn Reece, currently a South Carolina State Senator in the General Assembly, who owned the Krispy Kreme Donut store in Spartanburg, were going to be the other Democrat candidates who would file before the March 31, 1998 deadline. Thus, maybe I could get into runoff with one of these candidates. I fully supported Democratic Candidate Jim Hodges for Governor as he had permanent good strong environmental platform and pledged he would hold Industries to existing State and Federal

Environmental laws. Present Governor Beasley's stance was just the opposite. He didn't care how many citizens died. South Carolina Department of Health and Environmental Control had a bad reputation for the past ten years!

I wanted to find out how our U.S. Federal Political Process worked. I discovered that very quickly. Money buys votes. The one with the most money wins! So if you cannot afford the TV, radio advertising, other media exposure, mailers etc, you can't even come close. I only raised four thousand dollars. Whereas all the rest raised four hundred thousand dollars each! All the other five Republican candidates, whom I had debated close to five times, were going to have funds close to $300,000 to $400,000. I got in contact with a campaign consultant and fund generation expert in Washington, D.C. She had worked for the former U.S. Senator Bob Dole. Her name was Beth Gable of Gable Associates Inc. She said she would from her offices in Washington, D.C. try to raise campaign funds for my campaign committee. She sent me a commission fee agreement, which I signed, and agreed to give her an 8% commission fee on all funds she gathered. However she raised no money. It certainly seems like incumbents in these political offices hold impenetrable Superman positions. If you can raise the most money, then you can never be beaten.

Publicly Financing of U.S. Federal Election Campaigns:

For example, in the U.S. 4th Congressional District of South Carolina there are approximately 190,000 registered voters in Greenville County, approximately 125,000 registered voters in Spartanburg County, and approximately 70,000 registered voters in Union and portion of Laurens County in the 4th District (now these are 1998 figures) Thus, we have approx 385,000 registered voters in this U.S. 4th Congressional District.

What Congress should seriously consider is setting up completely public financing as follows:

U.S. 4th Congressional District of South Carolina

(1) That a federal tax of $5.00 per registered voter be assessed by U.S. Congress, and this would raise the $1,925,000 (385,000 Registered Voters in 4th District x $5.00)

That it shall be deposited with the S.C. Election Commission.

(2) That all Candidates who filed with the S.C. Election Commission between the Filing Dates of March 15, 2002, to March 31, 2002, would be eligible for their share of the public funds.

This would be said $1,925,000 divided by number of candidates filed.

(3) That the S.C. Election Commission would distribute on April 15, 2002, the specified Public Finances Portion as calculated from (2) to all the candidates.

(4) That all Primaries are eliminated. Since all primaries are eliminated all candidates would have the public financed money for entire campaign period. They would have the Public Financed Money to use until the General Election, the second Tuesday in November.

(5) Winner would be the one who got the most votes. Other facets of Election Reforms that I believe should be enacted are discussed. Congress should pass new legislation that authorizes magnetic strip magnetic voter cards Then all the registered voters in said "the Greenville Registered Voters Office, the Spartanburg Registered Voters Office, Union County Registered Voters and Laurens Registered Voters Office" who are in the U.S. 4th Congressional District would be processed "New Magnetic Strip Photo Identification Cards" With the Magnetic Identification that would coded with their New personal Computerized Voter Code.

That the Congress should pass into law that authorizes the S.C. Election Commission to be able to put these "New Magnetic Strip Voter Machines in various locations, banks, markets, etc. and Voter Registration offices for the entire four weeks before the General Election.

In the next two pages are two photos I took of Dorothy Love and political candidates. The first photo I took was of President Bush with his hands on the shoulders of my daughter, Dorothy Love Sanders. The second photograph shows Honorable U.S. Senator and Vietnam Veteran John McCain leaning down to shake hands with my daughter, Dorothy Love Sanders.

CLEAN WATER ACT U. S. FEDERAL ENVIRONMENTAL WHISTLEBLOWERLAWSUIT AGAINST U.S. EPA ADMINISTRATOR, SCDHEC, BOWATER CORPORATION AND INTERNATIONAL PAPER

I mentioned that I filed this Whistleblower Environmental Lawsuit # <u>7 : 01-1973- 13AK</u>

against the defendants April 21, 2001, in U.S. District Court of South Carolina,

Greenville

Division. I filed this suit as I was illegally fired from SCDHEC in December 1999. South

Carolina Chief Administrative Law Judge Marvin Kittrell had issued an Order in

September 1999 that Ordered SCDHEC and all its agents and managers, officials to stop

at once from issuing phosphorus limits in all NPDES permits. However, SCDHEC and its

managers felt they were above the law. They continued to add phosphorus limits in

several permits. I was ordered to write phosphorus limits for Rock Hill municipal

wastewater plants in criminal violation and criminal contempt of Judge Kittrell's Order.

Brad Wyche gave the order that I be criminally fired. I have proof from Mike Montebello that orders from Brad Wyche and Douglas Bryant were issued to criminally fire me. Magistrate Catoe dismissed my complaint on a corrupt technicality. The 4th Circuit Appeals Court in Richmond, Virginia, upheld the corrupt, illegal dismissals from the District Court, Greenville Division. My Writ of Certiorari #01-2219 has been up at the U.S. Supreme Court for over five years since February 2002. Below I'm going to summarize the case and it's still pending at the U.S. Supreme Court:

STATEMENT OF THE CASE

Shown on photograph 46, on preceding pages is photo of President Bush with his hands on the shoulders of our daughter, Dorothy Love Sanders.

Shown on photograph 47, on preceding pages is photo of Honorable U.S. Senator John McCain and 2000 Presidential Candidate shaking hands with our daughter, Dorothy Love Sanders.

On April 21, 2001, I filed this 7 : 01-1973- 13AK National Whistleblower Environmental Clean Water Suit against U.S. EPA Administrator, SCDHEC, Bowater and International Paper. The suit was filed in U.S. Federal South Carolina District Court, Greenville Division. Since I worked for SCDHEC for all of 1999, I had data, evidence, witnesses of the civil and criminal racketeering of many but including former SCDHEC counsel W. Thomas Lavender who moved over to Nexsen, Pruett, Jacobs , Pollard {that Lavender whose relative worked at Engelhard had informed all his clients "Anything You Want , You Got It!"} Of course, he meant if you come through us, Nexsen, Pruett, Pollard, LLC., we'll get you variances from all National & SCDHEC Environmental Regulations. Absolutely the Law doesn't apply to them! I also tried to get assess to the SC Administrative Law Courts and Judges. However, the SCDHEC current counsel,

154

Samuel Finklea III conspired with South Carolina Administrative Law Judge Ralph King Anderson and got him to change his ruling from open Court, and exempt the subpoenas of Commissioner Bryant, Brad Wyche, and others. Others had information on SCDHEC's criminal racketeering and their criminal contempt of Chief South Carolina Administrative Law Judge Marvin Kittrell's September 1999 ORDER.

This Whistleblower U.S. Federal Environmental Lawsuit was brought under current U.S. Federal Precedent Setting case as Follows: <u>Friends of the Earth vs. Laidlaw Environmental (120 U.S. Supreme Court 693, January 2000)</u> and this was and is U.S. Precedent case before Judge Joe Anderson, South Carolina District, Columbia Division, decided 7-2 by our U.S. Supreme Court in January 2000. Of course, note Chief Justice Roberts, your predecessor, Chief Justice Rehnquist was in the majority of seven.

Maybe God should send his Absolute Powerful Rod and Staff to you and the children and grandchildren of those who do not fear God. Some of you need to feel how the residents around Engelhard feel who have lost loved ones. Their loved ones have been criminal felony murdered by the criminal racketeering of Lavender, Finklea III, and the criminal racketeering of Engelhard officers and Engelhard Corporation for the past 18 years. And even though Paul Cavanaugh, criminal investigator for SCDHEC, has affidavits on Engelhard's criminal racketeering, nothing has been done! Even though Engelhard fired Paul Fryer, and Fryer filed U.S. Federal Lawsuit before Ross Anderson in the same U.S. Federal District Court, Greenville Division, and spent $55,000 of his own money, his case was dismissed on technicalities.

I, Launeil Sanders, also have filed formal affidavits before the S.C. Attorney General Condon on W.Thomas Lavender's racketeering. There is no justice for Paul

Fryer who has 'Platinosis Disease', and who could not get access to the U.S. Federal Courts, and who will die from his disease. And there is no justice for the many who have died of these deadly diseases and the many thousands who will die in the future.

For my Writ of Certiorari #01-2219 has been up to the U.S. Supreme Court since February 28, 2002 (five years). My Writ of Cert to U.S. Supreme Ct #01 -2219) National Whistleblower Environmental Clean Water Suit against U.S. EPA Administrator, SCDHEC, Bowater and International Paper was originally filed in April 21, 2001. Thus, our government cannot ever, including the U.S. Supreme Court, act in a reasonable time manner!

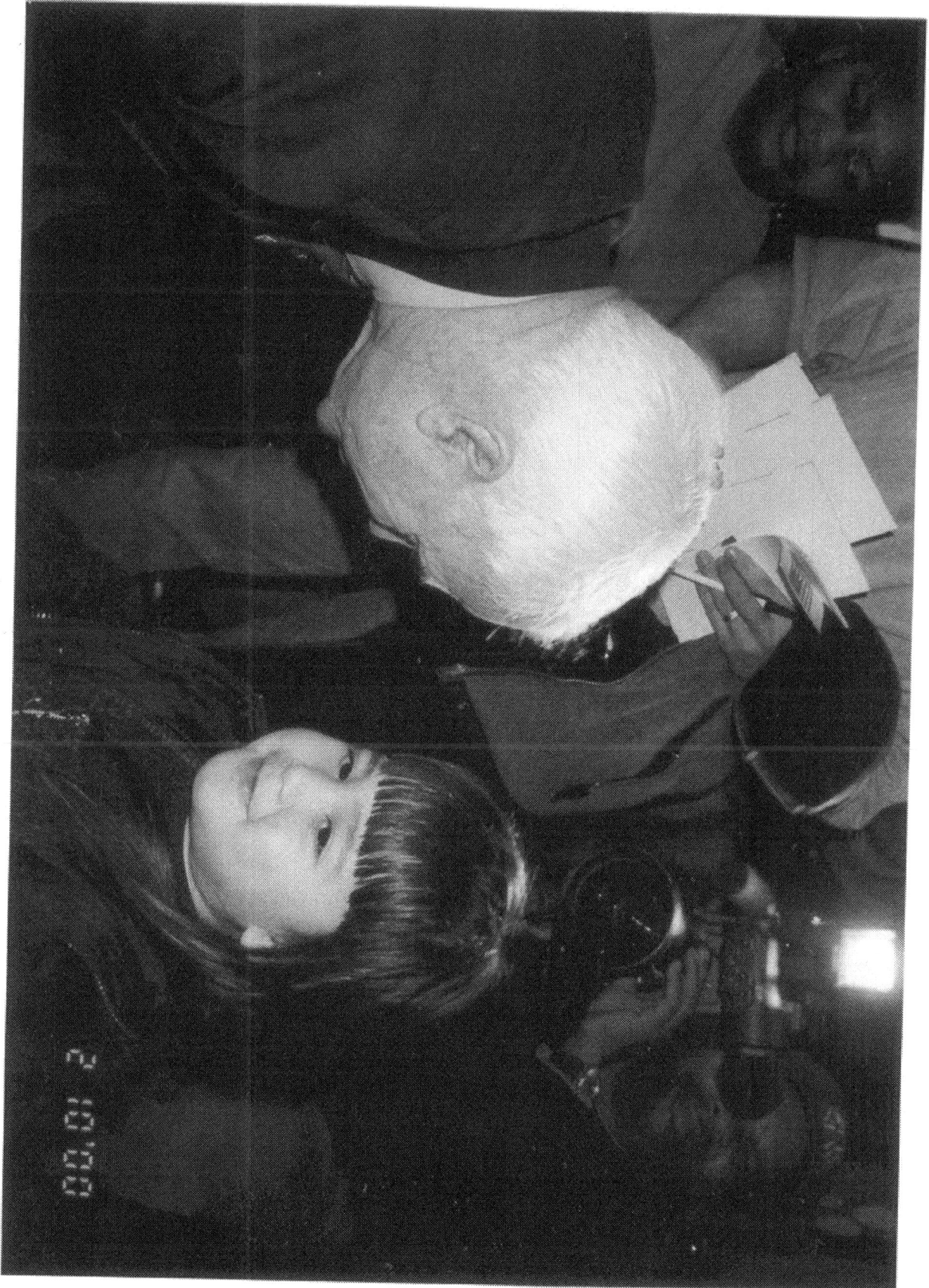

158

13

FIASCO OF MY U.S. PATENT APPLICATION WITH THE U. S. PATENT AND TRADEMARK OFFICE

I filed my U.S. Utility Wastewater Patent: "Raw Influent Treatment Processes Eliminating Secondary Biological Treatment" in April 1999; the fees were $925.00. The U. S. Patent examiner, whom I was assigned, was Peter Hruskoci. He sat on it for one year, and then requested I submit some new information. In May 6, 2000, I was requested to submit revisions. I submitted all revisions requested by Hruskoci on May 31, 2000. Then on October 6, 2000, he claimed that my U. S, Patent application of April 9, 1999, had been abandoned! Hruskoci and all U.S. Patent Examiners are required to rule on the patent applicability in 180 days. Thus, Hruskoci just disregarded my revised materials that I submitted on May 31, 2000. He made me pay the fees again for new patent application even though it was identical to the revised application under current U. S. Patent and Trademark Office (USPTO) laws. Thus, I had to pay new USPTO fees again of $975.00.

In October 30, 2000, I got a new U. S. Patent Application number; and Hruskoci had put into the USPTO Record that my initial filing on April 9, 1999, had been abandoned. From October 2000 until December 5, 2002, I had communicated with Hruskoci. I knew that my patent was patentable. I had to find a way to persuade him to understand the importance, absolute requirements of my proprietary devices. Hruskoci issued a final decision on my application, again denying my patent. The final denial had Hruskoci's boss, David Simmons name and telephone number. I immediately called David Simmons on December 8, 2002. Just as I had with Hruskoci, I tried to explain in very plain English details why my patent was patentable, and of the fact that currently there was "a criminal flagrant loop hole in the Biological Oxygen Demand test utilized by the sewage treatment plants and the 800 to 850 pulp and paper mills in America." I also tried to point out to Simmons that all of prior art issued by other examiners and Hruskoci were not being utilized in the industry. Simmons was completely obnoxious toward me. Simmons was hateful, odious, offensive and abominable. Simmons said "he was not going to issue my patent, and that I would only obtain a U.S. Patent if the USPTO Appeals Board issued my patent." Simmons said I made a severe mistake by not using one of their recommended patent attorneys. I told him I was going to respond to Hruskoci's final denial action, for which I complied. However, I had sixty days to respond; and I submitted all revisions and requests from Hruskoci. However, in July 2003 Hruskoci issued another abandonment saying I had not responded! This was an outright lie, and there was criminal misconduct by David Simmons, Hruskoci's boss.

After I appealed, in July 2004, the final decision of Hruskoci, I obtained an Appeals Petitioner Examiner named Douglas I. Wood. You will find out when you deal with any of our federal government agencies, they are inefficient, cannot do anything quickly and are totally insufficient. We, as Americans, have to demand changes and pursue that these changes are made. Right now, it seems to me you cannot fire any corrupt bureaucrat for any reasons. I paid to Douglas Wood the appeal fees of $165.00 and $665.00 for a total $830.00. And I sent my appeal documents as required in July 2004, Certified U.S. Mail, return receipt requested. So in almost two years later, May 2006, I inquired of my U.S. Senator Lindsey Graham to inquire at the USPTO of its status. You see, the USPTO has been sitting on my appeal for almost two years and have been criminally negligent. However, after I went to the bank, and pulled my cancelled checks in the amount of $830.00 to refute these USPTO lies. I drafted another letter to the USPTO.

My wife is sort of a pessimist, and I am an opposite, an optimist. She thinks that my U.S. Patent will never be issued. Of course, I really truly believe that it will be issued sometime in the future. In fairness to Janneth, she has seen my endless "denials and denied letters from the U. S. Patent and Trademark Office." But she knows it's been in God's will. Jesus told us to go out in the world and witness to people all around it! Jesus desire is for us to be obedient disciples and go out and bring the lost to Christ! And that's what I'm going to do! I'm going to remain standing in the gap for Jesus Christ!

14

MY MOTHER, DOROTHY SANDERS CRAIG COMES TO LIVE WITH US IN SOUTH CAROLINA

My Mother had married Harold Craig in February 1990. My sister, Janice Harden, had a terrific paroxysm, convulsion and fit because she knew Harold was not going to let her drag, haul around Mother with the chain on her neck. Sister had her son, Eric Rickman, living in Mother's house on Lakewood Drive, Memphis where we were raised. Eric Rickman was living in Mother's house free and not having to pay a cent of rent money! Harold suggested that Mother sell that house and get her child's share out of the house. She did that in or around 1996. As I detailed earlier, Janneth and I went to spend a few days with Harold and Mother in July 1994 when she was about four months pregnant with Dorothy Love. Harold had a massive stroke in October 21, 1994; he was moved into the Veterans Hospital and died on December 24, 1994. Harold never got to meet our gift of love from God, Dorothy Love Sanders, named after my Mother, born on December 26, 1994, two days after God called Harold home in "the twinkle of an eye." After Harold died and was buried, sister came back to put the chain around her neck and drag her around. Sister directed to Mother exactly what to do! Ann Harber, of Millington, Tennessee, knows how my sister treated Mother all those years after Harold died.

My sister, Janice Harden, desired to institutionalize my mother, Dorothy Craig, into a Tennessee institution home because she had Alzheimer's disease. Janneth and I agreed that Mother could come live with us. So Dorothy Love, two friends of mine and I went to Atoka, Tennessee, to move Mother to South Carolina. On or around June 3, 2003, we moved all of Mother's belongings and her to South Carolina. The next month in July 2003, I discovered that my sister had stolen some of Mother's money. Mother did not have a lot of money in the first place, but I knew my sister, Janice Harden's and my brother, George Larry Sanders' history. As within six months after the Dr. Charles Jarrett murdered my father in June 1982 by administering a criminal lethal dosage of Heparin and forcing a heart stroke and death, sister had taken $8500.00 and brother had taken $6500.00; and Mother only had $32,000. Thus, she would have been in bankruptcy shortly in 1982. In 1983, I set up a meeting; however they ran off and didn't want to meet with me. They had been caught, they would rather run off and hide! Now in 2003, my sister, Janice Harden, had transferred $13,000 of mother's money to her name, not jointly. And you see, I really found out the place my brother's and sister's hearts were grounded in 1983. Mother had never, ever managed money or finances in her life; but Mother was another of those God-fearing Americans who put God first in her life. Brother and sister knew they could go to the bank and borrow the money; however they knew they could take advantage of Mother and there was no one around to stop them. If my father were still alive, they would have been petitioning the bank for the money, which was the honorable thing to do. However, they chose the sleazy, dishonorable piece of sin way to do business with the flesh! I was disappointed, disgusted with my sister and brother in 1983!

Now here we are in 2003, and she had transferred $13,000 of mother's money to her name, Janice Harden, her social security number; and it did not have mother's name on the account. Mother called sister by telephone; and sister told mother and me that that money would always stay in Tennessee and she would never get that money! Dorothy Love who went with me to move mother to South Carolina had heard sister yell at me "If you don't leave mother's money alone, Larry and I will have you in court." She yelled this because mother closed out her Tennessee joint account with her the last day, before we moved mother and all her household goods to South Carolina. There were exceptions of household goods that were not moved to South Carolina. Sister and brother had tagged all items that they wanted, and we were not to remove them. You see, Mother was already dead to them; and they were prowling over the deeds of the flesh, the deeds of Satan, all the materialistic goods like corrupt voracious, ravenous, greedily, rapacious birds eating road kill along the highway. The exceptions were all tagged as mentioned with either sister's or brother's name on them. Of course, sister had already taken the antique sewing machine and other antiques to her home. She had the antique dining dresser, which was Dorothy Craig's Mother's, with sister's name on it! Maybe, when the rapture comes "in a twinkle of an eye" sister and brother will tag all these materialistic items to be raptured with them! I should tell you about when Dorothy Love and I went back to Millington, Tennessee, for mother's funeral on that July 14, 2004. Dorothy Love heard Troy Harden (sister's husband) telling me "well, we have been watching your

Mother die!" I would like to have the name of another God-fearing American couple in Millington, Tennessee, who are aware and did experience the treatment of mother by my sister. Their names are Jack and Ann Harber. Ann Harber and Jack Harber were friends of Harold and Dorothy Craig. That my sister simply hated Harold as when mother married Harold in February 1990, sister couldn't stand it! She attacked Mother in various ways. Here we are in 2003, and I have had all this experience in America's legal system, and I thought the system would work for my Mother. However that was a fatal mistake; as the premise always holds true, "If you go up against corrupt officers of the court, fatal attorneys who will do anything, violate the law, lie, incorporate their close friends, Judge Brasfield, who can be distorted easily, then you can do just about anything you want to!" And, of course, sister's attorney William Cole is another one of those "slippery slick willie snakes and scum sucking bottom feeding scavengers." In August 1994, the _USA Today_ published "Do you know the difference between a lawyer and a catfish? One is a scum sucking bottom feeding scavenger, and the other is a fish!" We are not going to bring back Mother from heaven; but someone has to stand in the gap to change the system!

So now you know sister has told Mother in July 2003 that she will never, ever get her $13,000, it will always remain in Tennessee in sister's bank account. But this is not all of the money that sister has stolen nor is planning to steal. As Mother and I find out in late July 2003, that sister had her sign a power of attorney to her. Now sister is going to sell the house and land for $85,000, out from under her, while she was in South Carolina. The house and land in Tipton County, Tennessee, is probably appraised for around $130,000 to $140,000. So, thus it seemed many corrupt deals were set up and is in the works since they (brother and sister) "have classified mother dead in their lives and let's get onto splitting the money from her house. Let's see how fast we can expedite getting our hands on rest of mother's money!" So on August 13, 2003, Mother, Dorothy Love and I drove to Tennessee to get an "A Power of Attorney and Living Will Provisions" signed by her on that August 13, 2003. And I drove to Tennessee the next day August 14, 2003, to get legal action filed for Mother. Sister and brother were properly legally served. However, that did not stop the William Cole from selling mother's house out from under her on August 28, 2003, while Mother was here in South Carolina with me. Tipton County Judge Brasfield is an intense rotten, impure agent. For remember I, Launeil Sanders, had August 13, 2003, "A Power of Attorney and Living Will Provisions" that legally entitled only me, Launeil Sanders, to make any decisions for Mother. It declared moot, invalid any previous power of attorneys signed by Mother. But just as shown to you when you have "slippery slick willie snake and scum sucking bottom feeding scavenger, William Cole, who knows he is above the law," he can do anything he wishes. And the corrupt Circuit Tipton County Judge, enables him to literally violate the law.

I also filed a formal affidavit with the U.S. Attorney General Roberto Gonzales on the criminal racketeering of Janice Harden, William Cole, Germantown Properties Inc. and their agent Lynn Craig and Marsha Brasfield. But as corrupt as our legal system is, I will be surprised if they intervene and do the Godly right thing! And I didn't see Lynn Craig, William Cole, or the corrupt Brasfield there at mother's funeral in Millington, Tennessee, on that July 14, 2004, three years ago. For when Mother went to the doctor here in Spartanburg, South Carolina, in July 2003, she weighed 151 pounds. Yes, does "the Janice Harden, the William Cole, the Lynn Craig and the Marsha Brasfield feel a

166

little bit guilty for execution of the criminal starvation down to 74 pounds and the criminal felony death of Dorothy Sanders Craig?"

Before I took Mother back to Tennessee for a visit on September 17, 2003, Mother signed a second "Power of Attorney and Living Will Provisions" with this second one signed on September 12, 2003, in Spartanburg, South Carolina. Now I have power of attorneys with living will provisions signed in both Tennessee and South Carolina. However, I again underestimated America's legal system and the corrupt attorney William Cole and Judge Brasfield. You would think for the sixteen years that I have been trying to access America's legal system, I would have learned that the first premise always holds true. That premise is "that Pro Se litigants can never access the system." The reason is that you have too many unscrupulous attorneys, and some of these unscrupulous, unethical attorneys graduate to become corrupt judges. For just as violence in our courts has been well reported, the root of all these killings, murders, the inhuman treatment by parties in domestic courts is all about the system! I really believe there are no Christian attorneys. Why should there be? *Our American Heritage of God* has been removed from our country! *Our American Heritage of God* has been removed from our public schools and thrown into the toilet! You have learned earlier that Cole and Brasfield are not the first tainted attorneys and judges that I have had experience with.

I listen to Dr. James Dobson's <u>Focus on the Family</u>, and I agree with his philosophy "For I wouldn't cast my ballot for one who didn't believe in the right to life." The right to life, as stated in other parts of my biography and the Bible and the Bible from Ruth as quoted in this biography "all our children are gifts from God." "When I'm just like I am walking down Calvary's path and hill, my feet are off the ground as Jesus

167

Christ is carrying me." Jesus Christ makes my life whiter than snow. God has sent me the vision, the Holy Spirit. God has promised to remove any obstacle in my life that would impair me from his will, His Godly plan for me. I promised God to have the courage, the patience, and the trust and faith to do His Will and that he would have Jesus Christ walk with me.

15

U.S FEDERAL LAWSUIT #04-2280-BN FILED IN WESTERN DISTRICT OF TENNESSEE, MEMPHIS DIVISION TO TRY TO PREVENT STARVATION OF MY MOTHER, DOROTHY SANDERS CRAIG

I knew that Mother was being starved to death, and only thing sister and brother gave a care about was how soon they could get their hands on the money. Love, peace joy and righteousness all come from God. But in America the $2000 per hour lobbyists; the rich greedy, voracious, avaricious corrupt oil companies that have fixed oil and gasoline prices; the rich, wealthy corporations who want to close all U.S. jobs and ship, outsource overseas all our jobs so that they can pay $ 0.15 per hourly wages are the ones in charge and the very ones who are running America. We, the citizens, sit idly by. Let's stop that and organize 2,500,000 disciples of America. We need real change in America. My wife in the Philippines made $2.50 a day or $0.30 per hour. Thus, I knew that Brasfield let

them sell Mother's house and land while Mother was living in South Carolina. It was not right, but it happened. The first basic premise of the Court always reigns supreme! If you have corrupt officers of the Court on your side, you never, lose. Mother's house was sold for $85,000, probably about $50,000 below its appraised value. However, I didn't know where the money was! Additionally, as demonstrated earlier, the house was sold for $85,000. I knew that I had the only two "Power of Attorney and Living Will Provisions" that were legal, the latest.

Shown on photograph 48, on preceding pages is photo of Janneth inside Mother red Austin Healey with Mother looking on.

Shown on photograph 49, on preceding pages is photo of Mother, Launeil Dorothy Love and Janneth at her home in Atoka, Tennessee.

Shown on photograph 50, on preceding pages is top photo of Mother sitting outside at her house in Atoka, Tennesse, opening presents at her 73 rd birthday in October 1993. The bottom photo is another photo of Mother holding Dorothy Love.

Shown on photograph 51, on preceding pages is top photo of Mother sitting on her sofa holding Dorothy Love at her home in Memphis, Tennessee. The middle photo from left has Launeil, Dorothy Love in the red wagon and Mother on right. The bottom photo has another photo of Mother with Dorothy Love on her couch together.

Thus, I drafted a lawsuit and I drove to Tennessee on April 21, 2004, and filed the suit. This was filed in U.S. Federal District Court, Western District of Tennessee, Memphis Division on April 21, 2004, almost 90 days before Mother was criminally starved to death. In U.S. Federal District Courts, you have to have the stamped Summons sheet from that Clerk of Court before you can legally serve summons on the defendants. All the U.S. Federal District Courts are different. However they are all the same. As they all across America never, never let Pro Se litigants access the system. The whole system is corrupt with triple agents. And if you or any of you 300 million citizens care about America, you had better rise up! Additionally, we filed a "Motion for Emergency Hearing Pursuant to 28 USCA Rule 12(d)." However you will see, no hearing was ever held, granted. The U.S. Federal Western District of Tennessee, Western Memphis Division, Judge Breen and all the employees, including Clerk Trolio, are all criminal accomplices to the criminal starvation of Mother, Dorothy Sanders Craig. The fate of my Mother was facilitated by all of you due to the criminal failure of the U.S. Federal Court and its employees! Judge Breen didn't even read the suit until 11 months had lapsed. Probably the corrupt Clerk Trolio is just as guilty and should be immediately fired!

The lawsuit we filed on April 21, 2004, was case # 04-2280-BN and Writ of Certiorari #05-5589, filed with U.S. Supreme Court on February 28, 2006. Of course, the suit was filed about 90 days before Mother was criminally starved to death. And the BN stands for Judge Breen. After mother was buried on that July 14, 2004, the next day on July 15, 2004, Dorothy Love and I went down to the U.S. Federal Western District of Tennessee, Western Memphis Division. We filed another emergency document, and notified the corrupt Clerk Trolio and this agent Judge Breen that mother was criminally starved to death and felony murdered and laid to rest on July 14, 2004. Just as I pointed out in this biography elsewhere, shortly afterwards, Janneth told me about the vision of "Mother coming into our bedroom saying to her she was in Heaven." Well, Clerk Trolio and Judge Breen, both of you should be removed from the federal court. Trolio should be fired immediately and disciplinary action investigated at once and considered for Breen.

After Breen dismissed our suit # 04-2280-BN on March 28, 2005, (now some 11 months after it was filed on April 21, 2004; as the corrupt misconduct by Judge Breen and the whole Western District of Tennessee, Western Memphis Division and Clerk Trolio), I immediately appealed it to the 5th Circuit in Cincinnati, Ohio. Judge Breen didn't even read the suit for 11 months. What kind of awesome, disrespectful, outright unrighteousness do you suspect this was? He could have prevented Mother's starvation and drugging, if it had not been for his misconduct and misbehavior. As there were never any hearings, and I appealed this case. I want some punishment for corrupt agents. I want all of the 300 million American citizens to know as I do "how ultimately corrupt, triple corrupt the America's U.S. Federal Courts are." Whether it's U.S. District South Carolina, Greenville Division; Western District of Tennessee, Western Division Memphis; the 4th Circuit in Richmond, Virginia; the 5th Circuit in Cincinnati, Ohio; or the U.S. Supreme Court in our nation's Capitol in Washington, D.C., there's no justice, righteousness or search for the Rule of Law in 99% of cases!" I want justice in America; but in man's law in America there is none. I don't want you to misinterpret me in this book. For I know my sister, my brother, many corrupt attorneys and many corrupt judges do not know God. I have the fruit of the spirit in my life as this morning in my communion with the Lord, he actually sent me the vision for he communed to me that it was in His Plan, our Holy Father's Plan, that I lost control of my biological children that Evelyn and I bore from God's will. When Bill Clinton sent the military in to re capture Elian Gonzales in Miami, I had mixed feelings. For I had my two biological children kidnapped from me; and mine were never returned. But God is in control; praise God that He is in control! And you know, I thanked God multiple times this morning for delivering me this vision in my silent moments with Him. I always want the power of the Holy Spirit to reign superior and to reign always in this earthly world until that rapture occurs. For if God asked me to sacrifice either of my current children, Dorothy Love or Colonel, or mine with Evelyn, I would trust in the Lord as our children are gifts from God and are on loan to us from God. I would plead and pray that my faith would be as strong as Abraham's in the test God had for him. For pastor Dr. Hank Williams preached in the fruit of the spirit. As preached by Dr. Hank Williams, "fruit of the spirit is identifiable in our lives by the power of the Holy Spirit! America needs genuine Christ like love for each other. That's real joy!" What God wants us to do is walk with Jesus Christ and, I believe, is to teach these 2,500,000 disciples and bring people all over the world to know the "Good News of Jesus Christ!" Glory, Glory, Hallelujah, Jesus Christ is Lord; Jesus Christ is Risen!

16

BREACH OF CONTRACT LAWSUIT AGAINST LANCASTER CONSTRUCTION IN SPARTANBURG COMMON PLEAS COURT CASE # 2002-CP-42-4224, FILED IN NOVEMBER 20, 2002

This case is on appeal to the South Carolina Appeals Court in Columbia, South Carolina.

This case is very, very important! Officers of the Spartanburg Court have perpetrated

severe misconduct. There are several aspects of this litigation which prove the

precedents, sovereignty discussed in this entire book as "If you go up against triple corrupt officers of the Court, no justice, truth, righteousness, and the Rule of Law is practiced!"

The basic premises hold true. If you go up against a devout racist attorney David Alford who never meets with you and your wife to prepare for the Jury Trial, and just steals your $1000.00 lawyer fees paid him, no justice may be obtained. And that he, Alford, is a racist who didn't meet with my wife or me to prepare for the jury trial. But he conspires with the opposing counsel, devout racist David Ingalls to jam out Constitutional Rights, Civil Rights, Due Process down our throats and deny our jury trial rights. After this two hours hearing called on August 8, 2005, our attorney David Alford was immediately fired and discharged. David Ingalls told Master in Equity, Cooper, that "Mr. Sanders' wife is a brown colored foreigner, and doesn't matter." And Cooper agreed and disallowed my wife, Janneth Sanders to come into the Master in Equity hearing on August 8, 2005, as only a two hours hearing notice was provided with Cooper's misconduct. My wife was at work and prohibited from coming into Court; and our jury trial in our case was jammed down our throats and illegally prohibited! Janneth Sanders, my wife, who is plaintiff in our civil action was at work and prohibited, restricted from coming into the Court. Also affidavits and formal written complaints by Janneth and I were filed with the Chief Disciplinary Counsel of South Carolina Supreme Court in August 8, 2005, against South Carolina racist attorney David Alford, South Carolina racist attorney David Ingalls, and against racist Master in Equity Cooper who committed severe racketeering for which some severe punishment should eventually be forthcoming.

But here in South Carolina the Chief Disciplinary Counsel of the South Carolina Supreme Court is a farce, a complete fraud on all the great citizens of the Great State of

South Carolina. For this Chief Disciplinary Counsel, Henry Richardson, of the South Carolina Supreme Court is a fraud, and doesn't intend to discipline nor sanction any triple corrupt attorneys or judges in South Carolina. For three of the South Carolina Appeals Court Judges, who are also racists, believe it's all right for our Constitutional Rights, Civil Rights, Due Process of our Jury Trial to be jammed down our throats!

17

DREAM TO ORGANIZE A CO-PRESIDENCY CAMPAIGN

Here it is 2006 and with all the happenings in the World, it seems that the return of Jesus Christ, our beloved savior is just around the corner. Tony Dale quotes in his God Fearing book "<u>Being</u> <u>Still</u> <u>and</u> <u>Knowing</u>", on page 45, "Tarry with him. That the word 'tarry' is such an elegant and simple picture of the state in which we need to be to receive His nurturing." I believe God brought two God fearing Americans into Janneth's and my life to help us in planning for our childrens' future. Tony Dale and Roland Stadelmann are those two individuals.

Tony Dale and Roland Stadelmann are two God fearing Christians who are both honest, decent financial planners who, I believe, you may trust. For Tony Dale has his own Capital Investment Companies, 175 Alabama Street, Spartanburg, South Carolina 29601. And Roland has his own Foothills Financial Group, 400 East Rutherford Street, Suite 310, Landrum, South Carolina 29356. Tony and Roland are definite assets in a very complex, constantly, changing America where the our government wants more taxes from you every day and currently taxes 85% of your Social Security retirement income. President Roosevelt, I'm sure, when he signed into law the U.S. Social Security Act never envisioned that it would be taxed at an 85% rate!

And you know I have probably shared with you previously in this biography what my fiancée who, of course, is my spouse, Janneth Sanders, now and is my lifelong God-fearing partner told me in 1993. Love, joy, peace, fruit of the spirit really does begin with God. I am living proof in this earthly world as God sent me a Christian lady from 12,000 miles on the other side of the earth, a place named Cebu, Philippines. I am living in this earthly world by the "grace of God." And in 1993, three years after my precious, previous spouse had died of liver cancer, I really needed a lot of the nurturing from our Lord.

Just as our pastor Dr. Hank Williams, Boiling Springs First Baptist Church preached "The Fruit Of The Spirit Is Peace", from Galations 5:22 and Philippians 4: 1-7. As preached by Dr. Hank Williams, "fruit of the spirit is identifiable in our lives by the power of the Holy Spirit! America needs genuine Christ like love for each other. That's real joy!"

From Philippians 4:1-7 from which Dr, Williams preached: "<u>Foundational Peace Principle</u>: the peace of God comes from God of peace and is the only true peace in life.

Peace is the presence of Jesus Christ. Peace is the absence of trouble." From Philippians 4: verse 2, "I beseech Euodias, and beseech Syntyche, that they be of same mind in the Lord." What the difficulty was between these two women of the Bible is not stated. However, what the Lord is saying "pursue harmony!" live in harmony with the Lord. From Dr. Hank Williams "Adam and Eve were in perfect harmony until they were tempted, and they ate the forbidden fruit. Adam and Eve destroyed the peace and harmony that they had with God. The first two people God put on this planet could not accomplish peace, love and joy through the flesh. We are the bride of Christ. The bride is spotless, living in the Holy Spirit and pursuing harmony and love. Practice Praising: Philippians: 4: verse 4, rejoice in the Lord always. Dr. Williams gave an example of the 35 feet to 40 feet diameter redwood trees in California. These redwoods have tremendous bark protections to have endured one thousand year storms and floods. Fire cannot destroy praise as it's your insulator to peace." How much praise do we as the 300 million citizens of America have in our hearts?

I really want to organize a Co-Presidency Campaign and organize two and one-half million disciples of our government. To do this, I realize it won't be easy. However, I know I don't have the money to perform this right now in 2006, nor do I know if the money could be raised. But I'm going to trust in the Lord, as I believe God will have Jesus Christ walk with us as it is time for God fearing Americans to stand in the gap and demand, take back our Constitution which our forefathers established some 230 years ago. As when the people rise up as one, peaceably unite, peaceably redress our government for our grievances just as stated in the First Amendment of our Constitution, the government will listen. For this Co-Presidency Campaign will have a woman and man running the entire campaign together, and with both the man and woman campaigning together, with both sharing in the political decisions, debates etc. I envision that this campaign should start around next July 4, 2007, Independence Day of 2007. That would allow about 15 to 16 months of campaign tour. It, if successful in winning the primaries and being nominated at the party convention in July 2008, would culminate in a 2,500,000 million disciples national march on the Washington mall in October 2008, in the second 2008 Saturday prior to the November 2008 Tuesday election. For our forefathers established our country to be a country of freedoms. And for the first time in hundreds of years the elected man and woman would serve together and sign the laws and would do everything as a team of two just like the husband and wife do in their God fearing family each day. For if elected in November 2008, it would really be a government "of the great people of the United States of America, for the great people of the United States of America and by the great people of the United States of America." For if God lets Jesus Christ walk with us, "no exceptions, no variances as everything is achievable through Christ. Come join us in this walk with Christ in reclaiming our fallen state!"

As Dr. Williams outlined additionally "Pray about everything and worry about nothing": Philippians: 4: verse 5-7 5) "Let your moderation be known unto all men. The Lord is at hand. 6) Be careful for nothing; but in everything by prayer supplication with thanksgiving let your requests be made unto God.7) And the peace of God, which passeth all understanding, shall keep your hearts and minds through Jesus Christ." "In verse five God is saying moderation is forbearance, tolerance. In verses 6-7 God is saying be careful for nothing. Then the peace of God (supernatural) will keep (guard) your feelings and

184

thoughts. Dr. Williams closed in "the talking parrot", for which the man bought at the pet shop. This is a real analogy of some of our earthly lives today. The parrot hadn't talked for a week, so the owner went back to the pet shop owner. The pet shop told him to put a ladder in the cage. But another five days went by and the parrot still hadn't talked. He went back to the pet shop, and pet shop owner told him to put a swing in the cage. But a few days later, the owner found the parrot almost dead, and he talked for the first time. "At that pet shop, do they have any food?" We should all pray cessantly as it says in the Bible; the peace of God surpasses human comprehension.

My dream is to organize these 2,500,000 million disciples from America with 50,000 coming from each state of the Union making up the two and one half million. I believe if we start in July 2007, we could use our internet web site to organize these disciples. Another fulfillment would be that we should tell all these disciples and announce that once elected; <u>we would cancel all state dinners at the White House.</u> I estimated that if we toured 850 of the disciples at the White House daily and 850 daily at the Capitol, then we could tour all 2,500,000 in the four years of the first presidency. Secondly, one husband and wife would be drawn randomly out of the daily 1700 to spend the night at the White House in the Lincoln bedroom, and one couple would be drawn to have lunch at the White House, and one would be drawn to have breakfast with the Co-Presidents. <u>And for all 1700 daily there would be dinner in the evening with honoring the disciples, teaching the disciples and preparing the disciples for their daily walks in their parts of our nation.</u> For 75% of America don't trust our 535 representatives in Washington. I believe this is the right way for America to take back our Constitution and to have more Christ like love, peace and joy to our nation's people. <u>But most important,</u>

this will be a campaign "of the great people of the United States of America, for the great people of the United States of America and by the great people of the United States of America."

Well, I have procrastinated getting my biography done as I've been working for 8 ½ years to obtain my U.S. Advanced Wastewater Utility Patent from the U.S. Patent and Trademark Office (USPTO) in Washington. And I've been trying unsuccessfully so far in achieving the U.S. Supreme Court to hear my U.S. Whistleblower Environmental Lawsuit Writ of Certiorari # 01-2219 that was filed at the U.S. Supreme Court in February 2002. However, from my actual experience, you cannot hold any bureaucrats in Washington responsible and accountable no matter how much criminal racketeering and criminal felonies they commit! But I'm going to try to get my biography published, and wherever some of my endeavors currently exist I will come back and issue a new book sequel. Hopefully, we will issue a sequel on the fifteen months' campaign.

18

CREATE 2,500,000 DISCIPLES OF AMERICA DURING A CO-PRESIDENCY CAMPAIGN

Now its Independence Day 2006, and I truly believe if we are to be successful in

achieving a Co-President's election in November 2008, we need to start soon. I feel that I

have been standing in the gap for our nation's environment since 1994, and that I'm the

only one who presently cares. However, I do realize that there are others who care about our environment. I'm sure if some of these who like the citizens around Lufkin, Texas, and Sheldon, Texas, who have filed suit in U.S. Federal District Court have found out just as I have. There isn't any justice or truth in our federal courts. Abitibi Consolidated Inc. discharges their treated wastewater in Texas from the Lufkin, Texas, and Sheldon, Texas mills just as all the other 850 pulp and paper mills in America. "A Matter of Justice" headquartered in Richmond, Virginia, is an excellent organization for which I have belonged. I believe they are all with great fortitude dedicated to returning the judiciary bureaucracy to the Constitution and Declaration of Independence that our forefathers executed some 230 years ago. Maybe if God is willing, some of those members will also sign up to be some of our 2,500,000 disciples of our government. All of the pulp and paper mills' treated wastewater is "black as your shoe, as black as your black sock." What we are really saying is the 850 pulp and paper mills are discharging a treated wastewater that is as follows:

3000 to 6000 milligrams per liter concentrations of COLOR

600 to 1000 milligrams per liter concentrations of Chemical Oxygen Demand, COD

300 to 600 milligrams per liter concentrations of Total Organic Carbon, TOC

I really thought and had high dreams in 1999 as I decided to apply for my U.S. Advanced Wastewater Utility Patent. I thought that in several years that I could obtain issuance of my patent from USPTO. However, I today over the past 7½ years have experienced reality; I still don't have my patent. Just as the God-fearing Tony Dale quotes in his book "Being Still and Knowing", on page 50 "Standing in the Gap, Intercessory Warfare. When you accept Christ into your heart, you are enlisting to fight in the oldest war on earth." I am ready to do battle against Satan and all the evil agents of the devil. As you notice I have been standing in the gap for Jesus. I know God had Moses tarry over in the wilderness for forty years until he learned to do it God's way and that God was satisfied that Moses was "certified, grounded, founded and rooted up in the word of the Lord." One has to be founded, grounded, and rooted up in the word of the Lord to do it God's way and be prepared to take on the pursuits of love, peace, joy and happiness. I told Tony Dale that God has had me over on the other side of the wilderness for the past 16 years in America's triple corrupt judiciary system; "so I guess God has me planned for 24 more years of on the job training in the judiciary wilderness."

I believe that most of America, probably 75-85% are really ready for some leaders who will lead from the heart. I have a vision that God wants all to be treated in a Christ like manner; he wants us all to be worthy of the walk with Christ. I'm not an expert on the Bible, and I really want to learn more each day of my life. I substitute in the schools a lot in the Spartanburg County public schools; I am in certified in science, math, biology, chemistry and physics. The other day when I substituted for the four year olds, pre kindergarten, one of the African American boys wanted me to read the Martin Luther King book to him; it was Martin Luther King day, January 2006. At the end of the day, he came by and thanked me for reading the book to him! That really made my day, and I thanked God for this witness today. When my daughter was in the fourth grade at Cooley Springs Fingerville Elementary School, her teacher was Mrs. Reams. When Dorothy Love and I visited one of the ladies in the hospital, Mary Cantrell, she was suffering a great deal. My daughter Dorothy Love is in advanced art class, and I asked Mrs. Reams if she would allow the class time to prepare get well cards for Mrs. Cantrell. Dorothy's class prepared her forty-two cards, and Dorothy and I delivered them to her. Mrs. Mary Cantrell is paralyzed in her legs, and she uses the metal braces and crutches to assist her in her walk. If we can get 50,000 government disciples from each state to sign up at our website, we really can make a difference and return America to our Constitution. God also has been taken out of our heritage; God was in our founding fathers hearts and we should reinstall our heritage as our forefathers desired. The first thing Thomas Jefferson did after the signing of the Constitution was to spend $25,000 of his own money and buy and distribute 45,000 Bibles to its citizens. As touched on earlier, we want to have all of these disciples participating in this Co-Presidency Campaign and help us win the primaries and eventual November Tuesday 2008 general election. And what we really want to do in late October 2008, as mentioned earlier, on the second Saturday before the November 2008 Tuesday election is to hold supper with the Lord that Saturday evening. We would invite all the parents, wives, loved ones of those 2650 servicemen and servicewomen who have died in Iraq. (presently in April 2007 over 3500 American soldiers killed in Iraq) We would invite all of those who have died in Afghanistan to sup with the Lord with these most distinguished guests. We would also invite all the soldiers injured and recovering from the Iraq and Afghanistan conflicts. (Approximately 25,000 as of January 2007) And we would charter buses from all the state capitols east of the Mississippi River on that Friday and pay for it with remaining campaign funds. You know, I guess that most of you who have children and have been to Disney World, have ridden the roller coaster that's in the dark called Space Mountain. One night God sent me a vision and it seemed like people, children were getting on the roller coaster ride that operated in the dark all the way. Somehow, in this vision, I could see that there was danger, travesty downstream at the end of the ride. I kept trying to tell officials, everyone I came in contact with, however "no one listened, and danger continued and I abruptly woke up from my dream." America needs new vision, new blood, new invigoration, new life that is blind to racist tendencies, color discrimination, sex discrimination, immigrant discrimination and the other violent tendencies of the flesh whom represent the devil. For the wealthy, filthy rich, and the ultra filthy rich lobbyists who make $2000 to $3000 per hour have flaunted with the devil to let the flesh rule in America. For it is my dream to start next July 4, 2007, and some of the platform issues are discussed below and items on how we could accomplish the big picture:

Next year's 2007 "A Capitol Fourth "celebration on the Mall next to the Capitol in Washington could be hosted by the man and woman and the variety of those supporting this dream. At this time it could be announced that this grass roots Co-Presidents Campaign would be launched! America is ready for this revolution for Taking Back our Country! The U. S. Parks Service, the National Endowment for the Arts, U. S. Army, PBS, and Lockheed Martin, sponsors the "Capitol Fourth Celebration". Jason Alexander was host on this past Tuesday July 4, 2006. Following are other parts of this strategy, as if we start in July 2007, then (some 17 months later) two Saturdays before the November 2008 election, we could culminate with the 2,500,000 government disciples march on the mall in preparation of the successful election of the Co-Presidents. Naturally, right now we would run as one has to be the Presidential candidate and the other the Vice-Presidential Candidate; however after swearing in on January 20, 2009, both would serve together all four years with the American Public seeing the man and woman performing America's duties as a team of two! Thus, I believe after the swearing in on January 20, 2009, the following Executive ORDERS would be signed by the Co-Presidents as follows:

1.   A National Energy Emergency is Declared; and that at once it is outlined how America becomes 100% energy self-sufficient in 2-4 years and eventually not import a drop of oil. Oil in Venezuela is five dollars per barrel with gasoline priced at the pump at $0.16 per gallon. In Saudia Arabia and Egypt oil is $20 per barrel, and gasoline is priced at the pump at $0.45 per gallon. So thus, part of the signed National Energy Emergency Declaration will include the following parts but not totally inclusive: (a) That by this emergency declaration and executive Order, America will fix, solidify, declare the price of oil that America uses after January 20, 2009, will be fixed at $22 per barrel. And all energy trading in America at its financial institutions will at once be suspended, and that no further energy trading is legally allowed in America until approved by the President (President and Vice-President now the Co-Presidents) or acts of Congress. And that any institution, party trying to sell, trade energy products other than the U.S. federal government will have all the force of the U.S. Justice Department brought upon them immediately investigating for criminal prosecution if warranted. Thus, oil companies (either domestic or foreign doing business in America) will only be able to charge $22 per barrel for all domestic oil being refined in this country; and additionally, in the executive order there will be provisions to prohibit U.S. oil companies from sending any oil or energy product overseas. And that the U.S. government will be the sole negotiator, purchaser of all foreign oil and or energy products for import into this country (b) Secondly, the President in the executive order will declare and release oil from the Strategic Petroleum Reserves to the U.S. refineries at the same $22 per barrel. And that

all the U.S. refineries and the pipeline transportation, gasoline terminals, and or the designated authority will release on a monthly basis to the U.S. Justice Department the wholesale price of gasoline delivered to each state; as at this price for crude the gasoline retail price should range in $0.55 to $1.00 per gallon. And the U.S. Justice Department will release to all major newspapers, media in every state the monthly wholesale price. Furthermore, the U.S. Treasury Department shall monthly print, release that month's daily raw oil and gasoline utilization; we are in this energy sufficiency together. (c) After signing the executive order by the Co-Presidents on January 20, 2009, the Co-Presidents will make a national address detailing the items, provisions discussed here and that will be detailed in the party platform. One is that all industry, and other large manufacturers utilizing large sums of crude oil shall be required to switch to coal. America holds 40% of the world's coal reserves, and we will utilize them to become 100% energy independent. Sufficient environmental controls are already required. Additionally all carbon dioxide gases control systems will be added (scrubbers will remove all carbon dioxide) so that gases are condensed, scrubbed, and carbon dioxide removed such as there will be zero pollution adding to greenhouse gases. I believe the re location of other industries next to major coal plants will be beneficiary to all industries as the pulp and paper mills will utilize all the scrubbing liquors as feed. Green house gases will be controlled. That additionally there will be Executive Order requirements that series of various industries will be located at the same locations of large power plants as pulp and paper mills will also be located at these locations to utilize the scrubber sulfur wastewater. That I mentioned to you earlier that I have an advanced wastewater utility technology patent pending that will save America's 750 pulp and paper mills ten billion dollars per year of electricity. However, detailed in other parts of this book, demonstrate how Washington bureaucrats have treated me in my eight and one-half years while struggling to obtain my U.S. patent and save America's pulp and paper mills ten billion dollars of electricity annually. And in the national address, we will ask all churches, religious groups and all other organizations who have church vans, vehicles etc. to organize church members to use the 8-15 passenger vans for work transportation of some of their members, where feasible, to save gasoline and numbers of vehicles in use. When I commuted 196 miles a day in 1999 from Spartanburg, South Carolina, to Columbia, crude oil prices were approximately $15-16 per barrel; and gasoline prices in South Carolina were $0.70 per gallon. It cost me then about $9.00 per day to commute, now with our gasoline prices up by 400 to 450%, that commuting would be impossible. When we built our house in 2003, OSB strand board was $5.10 per 4x8 sheet, now three years later it's$26.00 per sheet. Then plywood was $9.50 per sheet; now it's $37.00 per sheet. All our consumer goods, foods and everything are up 500% as America's goods are shipped by truck; so all America's citizens are paying 450% more because of the filthy rich, filthy wealthy lobbyists, oil and energy conglomerates who met secretly with Cheney. He promised, "we will get gasoline up to whatever you want it in America and we promise you are all free of any and all environmental litigation." Well, who do you think got the one hundred fifty billion dollars single-source Iraq contract after we got into the Iraq war? And the answer is Cheney's former corporation, Halliburton. And since Ken Lay was one of the persons who met with Cheney in his secret meetings "to sock it to all American consumers." And, of course, Ken Lay, just recently convicted of many criminal felonies in the criminal fall of Enron was one of those persons who secretly met

194

with Cheney. Did Cheney or Bush or any official at the now present administration come to the aide of the California consumers and citizens when Lay, Skilling and all of Enron were triple corruptly ripping off California and its citizens in 2001, 2002 for 41 billion dollars? The answer is no! Well, in Venezuela where gasoline priced at the pump at $0.16 per gallon and crude oil at five dollars per barrel. In Saudia Arabia and Egypt, gasoline is priced at the pump at $0.45 per gallon. There is truly something derived, rotten and corrupt with this philosophy of former oil executives now running our country and the Muslim countries now subsidizing their government oil, but corruptly ripping Americans off by $50-$60 dollars per barrel. In the 41 billion dollars rip off of California citizens by Enron Corporation, the only rhetoric that came out of Cheney and Bush and the entire administration was "that this was supply and demand and market forces at work." However, these were all out right lies. When Ken Lay died this past week, my wife cried out "that Christians don't get involved in depraved, tainted, defiled, vitiated, wicked, putrid, profligate, rotten criminal schemes to rip off California's citizens for 41 billion dollars. Christians don't get involved in corrupt schemes to rip off the Enron shareholders while selling millions of dollars of Enron stock options at 1000% profit margins prior to Enron 's bankruptcy filing." You know, the fact that Cheney paid this Iraq Chalibi a $3,500,000 monthly consulting fee out of U.S. taxpayer dollars, almost thirty –five million dollars is a total disgrace by one of our so-called leaders. (d) And also included in the National Energy Emergency and Declaration will be that an eventual U.S. Fuels Corporation will be signed into law by Congress within the first 120 days of 2009 where the U.S. Fuels Corporation will be 60% owned by the U.S. Government! And that Congress will outline how the private industries, public corporations will be allowed to participate in the remaining 40% ownership. First the government after January 20, 2009, will divert funds to start alcohol plants at all of the 850 pulp and paper mills in America. In addition, the executive order will state that 100% of the corn grown in America will go for America; none can legally be exported from this country. All of America's corn will go to the food chain or to produce ethyl alcohol for fuel for America's vehicles. And in conjunction with the large utilities, industries burning oil that are required to switch to coal, we will also be constructing Fisher Tropsh ™ or other processes to generate alcohol, gasohol from coal in the coal producing states and at large utilities who are burning coal. (e) And also included in the National Energy Emergency and Declaration will be that along with the U.S. Fuels Corporation will be signed into law by Congress within the first 120 days, that also the executive order will declare and will also be signed by Congress that after four years from January 9, 2009, that only vehicles manufactured and sold in America after January 2013 will have to include all the following, hybrid; and solar cells mounted on one part of vehicle (vehicle manufacturers to determine this in their testing whether it should be, hood, roof, trunk etc.); and that the vehicle design shall also be designed for 85% flex ethyl alcohol fuels. All of these are mandatory, and Congress should sign into law in the first 120 days of 2009. (f) That also in this Executive Emergency Energy Order will be that all planes of the U.S. government Agencies will be grounded and all required travel by U.S. Government employees shall be by U.S. Commercial Airlines. Only the planes governed by U.S. Homeland Security for America's Security would be exempted! This will save tremendous amounts of fuel and government expense. And if, elected, both of the Co-Presidents shall also fly with all the Commercial Airlines in as much U.S. Domestic travel as possible.

And in October 2000 I wrote a letter to South Carolina Governor Jim Hodges proposing a Repsol YPF refinery and pulp and paper cogeneration complex for the Charleston super port. Of course, I included the original also to Chief Executive of Repsol YPF. Governor Jim Hodges did nothing for the rest of his term. In 2003 Mark Sanford, Republican, took over from Hodges. I then forwarded this to Governor Sanford and his Secretary of Commerce. And again, it doesn't matter what your political party affiliation is; there are no God fearing South Carolinians who really care about its people. Sanford and his Commerce Secretary have done absolutely nothing.

2.   That Co-Presidents sign Emergency Declaration that *"Balanced Budget Amendment"* would be passed to the Constitution. The Bush/Cheney Administration has run this country into the ground with one trillion more in 2006 budget ($2,900,000,000 Trillion) verses the year 2000 federal budget of 1.8 trillion dollars. And it seems like Cheney has been the President for the past six years! Maybe it is Cheney and Karl Rove who have served as President the past six years.

3.   That 75% of America don't trust the 435 Representatives and the 100 Senators. This is ripe for two God-Fearing Co-President's Candidates to run a grass roots campaign. I guarantee you all, if we do not gain enough momentum to win in November 2008, we could positively win in 2012.

4.   Again I truly believe that just I have heard others say, "America needs true leaders who would rule from the heart!" Yes, they are right, and it is God's will that this be undertaken to get back to the Constitution for which our forefathers, drafted, designed, executed, and that many died for!

5.   <u>Of course, the first item of our Platform would be that we would have all of our</u> <u>troops out of Iraq in the first 100-120 days of 2009. And on that January 20, 2009, after</u> <u>the swearing in, the President brings all troops home from Iraq in exactly 100-120 days.</u> This would be the executive order signed. And with respect to Ken Mehlman, Chairman of the National Republican Party, prior to the November 2006 Election, he should have been fired! Praise God that now he has been rightfully fired. For in the Vietnam after the stable government was placed in effect, operation in 1967, there were after 1967 almost 39,000 soldiers killed of the 58,256 killed in the Vietnam War, and whose names are printed on the Vietnam War Memorial. There are many Vietnam Veterans who don't like the government lying to us then, and certainly don't like a repeat of the same lying from our government officials. You see, Mr. Melhman, evangelist Billy Graham, after his visit to Vietnam, went directly to President Nixon and urged him to end the Vietnam War as soon as possible. So, Mr. Melhman, "we did not cut and run in Vietnam." The Vietnam War destroyed Lyndon Johnson, as he knew he should have acted properly and prevented thousands of American soldiers' lives. But, Mr. Melhman, of whom you are also probably a draft dodger and never served a day in the American military, made a drastic mistake in those corrupt inaccurate statements on MSNBC's <u>Hardball</u> and <u>Countdown.</u> The 58,256, who so honorably died for our country in Vietnam, and all the fighting men and women who have died for our great country died for our Constitution and Declaration of Independence and for the freedoms and principles our country was founded. Congressman John Murtha of Pennsylvania, who is a highly decorated Vietnam Veteran, and the ten retired Generals who criticized Rumsfeld and Cheney, didn't have this corrupt "cut and run rhetoric philosophy." Your triple corrupt statement "that we

didn't want to cut and run in Iraq like we did in Vietnam" was reprehensible." You should have been directly fired then. Well, all of you who are responsible for this "cut and run rhetoric," stop at once. For it seems that drunkard Dick Cheney has been President and is running the Presidency. It is public record that Cheney was caught several times DWI in his college days. However, when he gets drunk on a bird hunting trip in Texas, and he shoots one of his Republican associates in the face, he is exempt from taking a police breath analyzer test. That is, which has been prevalent in this Cheney/Bush administration; they believe themselves to be above the law. Well, it's now after the November 7, 2006, National Election; and Ken Mehlman is toast! For Rumsfeld has not been fired yet, even though he has committed severe catastrophe mistakes costing many of the 2650 lives lost in Iraq (over 3000 now in January 2007) Rumsfeld should not have been chosen; however after he and Bremmer disbanded the Iraq army guard in April 2003, he should have been immediately fired. That I don't hear Bush, Cheney or Rumsfeld telling the American people, taxpayers and voters about the "eight year war" that Iraq and Iran waged for eight years. And, of course, during the eight year Iraq-Iran War, we, the United States of America backed, aided Saddam Hussein and Iraq! And were you told that Iran lost one million of its citizens during this eight year War! Have Bush and Cheney told the truth that we have made the entire Middle East worst off? Have they told "America" the truth about the Muslim Shiites who now have been put into power in Iraq and are Shiite Muslims? Have they told America the truth that Hezbollah Shiites are part of the Shiites of Iraq and Iran? Have they told the truth in that Hezbollah's leader, Sheik Sayed Hassan Nasrallah, is a Shiite, and completed his Seminary education in Iraq. What Iran couldn't do, achieve in their "eight year war" with

Iraq, America achieved that for them as the Shiites in Iran and Iraq are now united in the Middle East. Again, Iran lost approximately one million of its citizens during their eight year war with Saddam Hussein and Iraq! Cheney, Rove, Rumsfeld and Bush's sovereign invasion into Iraq was wrong, however God is in Control! God is in Control and the author of all happenings. I'm thankful and know that God is always in control. God has allowed this to happen as in His plan. Maybe God wants the Shiites to be in charge after hundreds of thousands of years of Sunni rule. We have got to elect some American leaders who truly care about our Constitution and about the dignity of all people, no matter what your race, national origin, sex and color consist of. We and I worship the "Prince of Peace." Have they told "America" the truth about Usama Bin Laden? There are exact differences in the Middle East Muslims as Sheik Nasrallah and the Hezbollah are as stated, Muslim Shiites and Usama Bin Laden and his Arab groups are Muslim Sunnis? As stated earlier, we don't have any real leaders in America, and the invading of a sovereign country Iraq in 2003 was misguided, however it was in God's Plan. And I will bet you that Rove, Bush, Cheney, Rumsfeld and all the hawkish power brokers who wanted war have not attended any of the over 3000 funerals of our Veterans coming home in body bags since 2003. As a matter of fact, on CNN's "***Larry King Live***" the other evening "Bush said he had never attended any of the funerals." And it's been the same Bush and Cheney administration that prevented the media from photographing these draped bodies coming home from Iraq and Afghanistan.

5.   I believe that I do know how to solve the "immigration issue" in America. Just as discussed earlier if we do it God's way, Christ will walk with us and anoint us with his blessings. My wife is a U.S. Naturalized American sworn in and naturalized in June 5,

1998, at U.S. Haynesworth Federal Courthouse in Greenville, South Carolina. In America, we know about immigration issues. After Janneth was sworn in as a U.S. Naturalized citizen, it took us three, 3, years to get her parents visa approved and about $1500.00 of fees to the old Immigration and Naturalization Service (INS) for her parents to arrive in America. Janneth's parents arrived to America on January 16, 2001, about nine months prior to 911. Her parents by the U. S. Citizenship and Immigration Service (USCIS), reorganized after 911 by U. S. Homeland Security, have had to reside in America for five years before they could apply for their Naturalization. In April 2006 they filed the N-400 Naturalization Applications and their fees were $400 each with a total of $800.00. August 1, 2006, I took them to Charlotte, North Carolina's Homeland Security office, for their fingerprints. Hopefully, they will be sworn in at a U.S. Federal Courthouse Naturalization ceremony before the end of 2006. In January 12, 2007, Janneth's parents were sworn in and Naturalized at the U.S. Citizenship and Immigration Service in Charleston, South Carolina. In 1993 when I filed for Janneth's visa to come to America, I found how time-consuming, cumbersome, wieldy and unmanageable the U. S. Immigration and Naturalization Service procedures were. Janneth's mother and father raised a daughter for over 70% of her life whose biological father abandoned her and her biological mother gave custody and guardianship to Janneth's mother and father. Recently my wife's petition to Homeland Security's District Director in Atlanta, Georgia, was denied. Her petition to internationally adopt this daughter and to have her classified as an immediate family member was, I believe, illegally denied.

Now, on January 12, 2007, Janneth's parents, Antonio Emberador and Juanita Emberador, have become citizens. The WCSC television (TV 5), local CBS affiliate in

Charleston, South Carolina, covered the ceremony and performed personal interviews of Janneth's Mother and Father. WCSC interviewers asked Antonio and Juanita "how does it feel to be an American Citizen?" As in most of these international adoptions, naturalizations, alien cards, visas etc, or in anything you want from the U.S. Citizenship and Immigration Service, the basic premise is if you have an attorney representation, you can obtain anything you want. For the nineteen, 19, Arab hijackers (who were all Saudia Arabia Sunnis) who crashed Boeing 757 jets into the two World Trade centers and the Pentagon in Washington were from Saudia Arabia. And because of the heroic heroes on the United flight that departed from Newark Airport, the hijacked jet plunged into the field in Pennsylvania instead of the White House or the Capitol. Well, I guarantee you Clinton's immigration policy was a mighty failure; and I guarantee you all nineteen, 19, Arabs from Saudia Arabia utilized an attorney and got everything they wanted! Basically, America does have too many attorneys; all the corrupt attorneys should repent, get saved. If not, they should find themselves a new profession. If they do not, then in January 2009 we are coming after them. After we reach them, our proposals to make America a better, integrity America will be presented to them!

19

AMERICA IS READY

Through out this biography I have shared some of my earthly experiences. I have also touched on some of my Godly experiences, and that I am fully committed to stand in the gap for Jesus. I was born in the South in Tennessee where racism, racial bias was rampant. However, even though things have improved, there are still many racists in South Carolina and America. Even in Tampa, Florida, where I was working in 1992 to 1993 at Raytheon Engineers and Constructors Inc., one of the engineer associates, after I showed him a picture of Janneth, asked "What did my mother and father think of me marrying a lady from the Philippines?" What he meant by that was his racial slighting against any other race other than his, Caucasian. Only God knew what was in Janneth's heart; but as you have discovered in these chapters she told me she was a Bible Baptist Christian. I thank God for the Free Will Baptist Ministry and Church of Independence, Missouri, for whom started a Baptist ministry in Cebu, Philippines, and that Janneth was baptized in this ministry as a Christian. Just as God sent me this Christian lady in 1993 into my life, I was committed to try to get her to marry me. I've told the story many times, and I have all of Janneth's cards she mailed me to Tampa, Florida, while we were writing each other. Once she mailed me her first card, told me she was a Bible Baptist Christian and enclosed a couple of photographs, I knew God had sent me a God fearing Christian lady from half way around the world. So it was up to my commitment to not let God down and get her to marry me. I would like to summarize these, and you know that I was in love with Janneth Emberador, prior to meeting her in Philippines in May 1993. Janneth Emberador Sanders, is my lifelong God-fearing partner. Janneth stated she put God first in her life, and that she didn't like drunkards, drug-addicts or gamblers as they would worship those vices. Furthermore, Janneth and I plan to lead a mission trip to Cogon, Dumanjug, Cebu, Philippines in the summer of 2008, if possible. Our pastor, Dr, Hank Williams of Boiling Springs First Baptist Church told us to pray a lot about the mission trip. For twelve years we have contributed to two Philippines pastors in Cebu, Philippines. Pray for us that this mission trip will maybe lead to construction of a church for Pastor Billy Payeo of Dumanjug, Cebu, Philippines.

As when Janneth sent me her first card and two photos, I was working in Tampa. And I immediately went to the store in Tampa, and bought her three birthday cards and three Valentine cards and express mailed them to her in the Philippines. I know God sent Jesus Christ to walk with me during my first visit to meet her in the Philippines in April and May 1993. My two and half weeks in the Cogon, Dumanjug, Cebu, Philippines was the best that I had ever spent. I wanted to convince Janneth during the two weeks visit in May 1993 that I was in this for the long haul. I really was in love with her; we were abstinent and waited until she got to America, and we were married in America in Atoka,

Tennessee. That I maybe got a few kisses in the Philippines, got to meet her parents, got to meet all her other relatives, got to go to church with her, got to go on long walks with her, got to go swimming in the ocean, Paradise Valley, and White Sands Beach, Philippines. And I got to enjoy the great Philippines cuisine and got to have the time of my life in fellowship with the one God had brought me. We did not consummate our Godly marriage until the night of February 26, 1994, after we were married in mother and stepfather's church in Atoka, Tennessee. I wanted God to bless us with children, if it was God's will. That in the Bible, from Ruth 4:13, "So Boaz took Ruth, and she was his wife: and when he went in unto her, the Lord gave her conception, and she bare a son." The Lord gave her conception; here Ruth had been childless during her marriage to Mahlon. Here is the true Biblical meaning, as all our children are gifts from God. This needs to be reemphasized in our modern world. I know God gave us our children just as in yours; all our gifts come from God just as our children are our most precious gifts. Maybe God will bless Janneth and I again, and we can have another child, maybe in Washington, if it is God's will. You know I am always astonished by the word of God; I get excited, I get nourished, I want to give all my obedience and be committed daily to a communion with the Lord. When God promised Abraham and Sarah a child, you have to be astonished for Abraham who was 100 years old and Sarah about 85 in years! What a magnificent feast before the Lord for God to grant conception to Sarah and for Abraham to become a father at 100 years old. God has blessed me also with the gifts of having children in my older age, and the blessed gift from our Holy Father of being an earthly father again. May God Bless all of you parents in America, and may God send Jesus to walk with you daily; and may he bless you and lead you to seriously think about becoming one of the two and one-half million disciples we wish to organize for America.

Of course, it is my dream to participate in this Co-Presidents grass roots campaign, as I believe it's what God wants for America. I, as you have experienced, never ever blamed God for my trials and tribulations; I have kept my faith and am ready to take on the battle against Satan. I genuinely want inspired leadership for America; all born again Christians are genuine. My wife is one of those genuine Naturalized Americans. And all of us who are natural born Americans love America. Janneth and I know that Dorothy Love and Colonel Launeil Tony are our two gifts from God. My allegiance is to God, country and family. You know, our country has such rich heritage; one where the South was one that had slaves, slave owners, rich plantation owners, an industrial revolutionized North and in 1860's a Civil War where over one half million of Americans gave their lives. It really has only been about forty years since our Congress signed the Civil Rights Act of 1964. The South has changed enormously as the South has undergone an industrial revolution, and many have migrated from the North to live in the Southeastern and Southwestern part of our country. Janneth says one of the best things she loved about America when she sat foot on American soil in 1994 is that our freedom country has many, many churches. America really has some genuine Godly heritage as God has been and is still in control. Just as the Honorable evangelist Billy Graham, after his visit to Vietnam, really saw what the problems were. Our American government officials lied to us for many years. He went directly to President Nixon, and pleaded with Nixon to bring our troops home and end the Vietnam War. You know we don't have any real leaders in America and the world. The real genuine question is will we and when we try to elect leaders who are committed to genuine peace. We as those who have accepted Jesus Christ as our personal savior do worship the "Prince of Peace." When do we elect real leaders who worship the "Prince of Peace" and walk with the disciples each and everyday! Our leaders, cannot be found. Where is our Congress?

It's all about the criminal theft, fraud and corrupt criminal racketeering by Enron officials, the giant oil companies to fix oil and American gasoline prices, which I have previously discussed. We definitely have to have new blood in the Presidency and Vice-Presidency, which we feel after election in November 2008 things will really change for all Americans. For it is well documented on Enron's criminal convictions of Ken Lay and Jeffrey Skilling a few months ago, the death of Ken Lay a week ago, and pending sentencing of Skilling in October 2006. Janneth and I conversed on Lay's death being announced on the evening news the other night; we felt again genuine Christians don't get involved in criminal racketeering and theft of 41 billion dollars from California's citizens and taxpayers. This morning I asked my wife, "what do you think gasoline prices were in 1974?" I was working in Charlotte, North Carolina. I remember the "corrupted gasoline fix is in by the oil giants and our government" as gasoline prices were at $0.30 per gallon. President Nixon caved to the oil company giants; and gasoline tripled in price to $0.90 per gallon in only three days. And the real corrupt collusion between government and industry oil giants was the following collusion: In Charlotte and I, believe, all the rest of the cities in America they, government and our big oil energy giants "made us line up in our cars, vehicles lines for four hours to get $5.00 of worth of gasoline. However, immediately two days later, after the gasoline prices were raised 300% to $0.90 there was plenty of gasoline." There was never any shortage, just a criminal fix. There was no gasoline shortage in 1974. And as discussed earlier in America and South Carolina the price of gasoline was $0.70 per gallon in year 1999. As soon as Cheney/Bush got in from year 2001 there has been 350%to 400% increase in gasoline prices. "If you don't believe that the oil giants with the cooperation of our government have fixed oil and gasoline prices to their advantages, then you would think there are no nuclear bombs in the world." In 2003 just three years ago gasoline prices here in South Carolina were $1.00 per gallon; now some three years later prices are $3.00 per gallon. Absolutely, the oil giants have merged (Exxon colluded with Mobil to become Exxon Mobil, Chevron colluded with Texaco to be one big Texaco); they have eliminated, squashed their competition and have no competition presently. In fiscal year 2005 Exxon Mobil made about 40 billion dollars of profit. And, I believe, the Mr. Raymond, former Chairman and CEO, in retiring, took approximately 500 million dollars, for which all was corruptly gouged from America's taxpayers. There are several items that need to happen to get America back on the right track; the 500 billion dollars through July 2006 that we have spent in Iraq has to end immediately. As we lost 58,256 American men and women soldiers in the Vietnam War and our leaders lied to us for many years. We probably will lose around 5000 to 10,000 American men and women soldiers in the Iraq War before we get all our 135,000 troops (now 170,000 troops in April 2007) out of Iraq. We will have with entirety all of our troops home by May 2009, and we will throw the greatest homecoming and Lord's Supper for all. We will definitely remove all our troops as detailed earlier in the first 120 days of 2009. We respect all 58,256 soldiers who died in Vietnam and all our soldiers who have died in conflicts and wars. Just as we proposed earlier, in that if we are successful in the year 2008 primaries to get nominated, we will have sup with the Lord the second Saturday before the November 2008 general election. And our distinguished guests will be loved ones of those who gave their lives (those who gave all) in the Iraq and Afghanistan. Additionally, all those who have been wounded, lost limbs, and have other wounds from these conflicts will be our distinguished guests! You know, there is only one person serving in our 535 representatives and Senators in Congress who has a loved one serving in our armed services in Iraq or Afghanistan, and you cannot know who that is even if you search for it! I don't see either of George W. Bush's daughters serving our country; nor is Cheney's lesbian daughter serving in America's military, nor did draft dodger Dick Cheney ever serve in America's military. (But Cheney received several deferments during Vietnam! Thus, don't you think it was a criminal crime for Cheney and Rumsfeld and the rest of the hawks to fabricate all the weapons of mass destruction and orchestrate our entry into Iraq? And don't you think they should be booted out for the betterment of the world and America? Cheney is a draft dodger, and the fact that Rove and Cheney have been President is why Rumsfeld has never, ever been fired! (Written previously before November 8, 2006!)

In the Bible, it says pray constantly, never stop praying. Come join us for this walk for America; for the Co-Presidents campaign will be one "<u>of</u> the great people of the United States of America, <u>for</u> the great people of the United States of America and <u>By</u> the great people of the United States of America." The government belongs to the people. We really should cancel at once all state dinners at the people's house "the White House." And as we tour 1700 of America's disciples daily in the four years; have dinner, supper for the 1700 daily; have one husband and wife couple selected to spend the night in the Lincoln bedroom at the White House every evening and have breakfast with the

Co-Presidents. May God Bless you in all your endeavors; and I would like to share with you one of my favorite passages from Isaiah 40:31 "But they that wait upon the Lord shall renew their strength; they shall mount up with wings as eagles; they shall run and not be weary; and they shall walk, and not faint." In these verses Isaiah 40:27-31, God is saying "Contrary to Israel's complaint, God is not too great to care (v.27). He gives power to those who wait on or hope in him (v.29), and they exchange (renew) their strength for his. (v.31)

20

AFTERMATH AFTER THE NATIONAL NOVEMBER 7, 2006, ELECTION

You know, throughout this biography I have conveyed to you, having experienced the Vietnam War, I was really concerned about going into Iraq in March 2003. I felt it might be another Vietnam War. But surely if it were, it wouldn't take God-fearing Americans that long to rally in the streets, Peaceably Redress your Government For Your Grievances and change America's course! Whoops, remember, I have stressed to you in my memoirs that I have sixteen years experience in America's judiciary, and you really don't have those First Amendment Rights to "Peaceably Redress your Government For Your Grievances." The 'greatest television show is MSNBC's Keith Olbermann's <u>Countdown.</u> Keith's show should be mandatory for all God-fearing Americans who care about America and our Constitution and principles, values for which our forefathers founded our country!

That's why I would like to quote one of Keith's special comments he has previously made. You may go to MSNBC's <u>Countdown</u> website and read all the worthy special comments Keith Olbermann made in 2006 and here in 2007. This special comment Keith made on the eve of our National Election on Monday, November 6, 2006. This special comment by Keith on 'checks and balances' is as follows:

"We are, as every generation, inseparable from our own time. This is our perspective, inevitably that of the explorer looking into the wrong end of the telescope.

But even accounting for our myopia, it's hard to imagine there have been many elections more important than this one, certainly not in non-presidential years.

And so we look at the verdict in the trial of Saddam Hussein yesterday, and, with the very phrase "October, or November, Surprise" now a part of our vernacular, and the chest-thumping coming from so many of the Republican campaigners today, each of us must wonder about the convenience of the timing of his conviction and sentencing.

But let us give history and coincidence the benefit of the doubt—let's say it's just "happened" that way—and for a moment not look into the wrong end of the telescope.

Let's perceive instead the bigger picture:

Saddam Hussein, found guilty in an Iraqi court.

Who can argue against that?

He is officially, what the world always knew he was: a war criminal.

Mr. Bush, was this imprimatur, worth the cost of 2,832 American lives, and thousands more American lives yet to be lost?

Is the conviction of Saddam Hussein the reason you went to war in Iraq?

Or did you go to war in Iraq because of the weapons of mass destruction that did not exist?

Or did you go to war in Iraq because of the connection between Iraq and the al-Qaida that did not exist?

Or did you go to war in Iraq to break the bonds of tyranny there, while installing the mechanisms of tyranny here?

Or did you go to war in Iraq because you felt the need to wreak vengeance against somebody, anybody?

Or did you go to war in Iraq to contain a rogue state which, months earlier, your own administration had declared had been fully contained by sanctions?

Or did you go to war in Iraq to keep gas prices down?

How startling it was, sir, to hear you introduce oil to your stump speeches over the weekend.

Not four years removed from the most dismissive, the most condescending, the most ridiculing denials of the very hint at, as Mr. Rumsfeld put it, this "nonsense."

There you were, campaigning in Colorado, in Nebraska, in Florida, in Kansas—suddenly

Turning this 'unpatriotic idea' into a platform plank.

"You can imagine a world in which these extremists and radicals got control of energy resources," you told us. "And then you can imagine them saying, 'We're going to pull a bunch of oil off the market to run your price of oil up unless you do the following."

Having frightened us, having bullied us, having lied to us, having ignored and rewritten the Constitution under our noses, having stayed the course, having denied you've stayed the course, having belittled us about "timeliness" but instead extolled "benchmarks," you've now resorted, sir, to this?

We must stay in Iraq to save the $2 gallon of gas?

Mr. President, there is no other conclusion we can draw as we go to the polls tomorrow.

Sir, you have been making this up as you went along.

This country was founded to prevent anybody from making it up as they went along.

Those vaunted Founding Fathers of ours have been so quoted up, that they appear as marble statues: like the chiseled guards of China, or the faces on Mount Rushmore. But in fact they were practical people and the thing they obviously feared the most was a government of men and not laws.

They provided the checks and balances for a reason.

No one man could run the government the way he saw fit—unless he, at the least, took into consideration what those he governed saw.

A House of Representatives would be the people's eyes.

A Senate would be the corrective force on that House.

An executive would do the work, and hold the Constitution to his chest like his child.

A Supreme Court would oversee it all.

Checks and balances.

Where did that go, Mr. Bush?

And what price did we pay because we let it go?

Saddam Hussein will get out of Iraq the same way 2,832 Americans have and thousands more.

He'll get out faster than we will.

And if nothing changes tomorrow, you, sir, will be out of the White House long before the rest of us can say we are out of Iraq.

And whose fault is this?

Not truly yours. You took advantage of those of us who were afraid, and those of us who believed unity and nation took precedence over all else.

But we let you take that advantage.

And so we let you go to war in Iraq to oust Saddam or find non-existant weapons or avenge 9/11 or fight terrorists who only got there after we did or as cover to change the fabric of our Constitution or for lower prices at The Texaco or …?

There are still a few hours left before the polls open, sir. There are many rationalizations still untried.

And whatever your motives of the moment, we the people have, in true good faith and with the genuine patriotism of self-sacrifice (of which you have shown you know nothing), we have let you go on making it up as you went along.

Unchecked and unbalanced.

Vote."

This special comment by Keith Olbermann on November 6, 2006, Election Eve is one of the many great special comments delivered by Keith and his crew! Keith Olbermann and his crew are all God-fearing Americans! May God continue to have Jesus Christ walk with all of you?

In summary, after the election, as we all know the day after, Bush fired Rumsfeld. But what about all the campaign jargon in that Rummy would be here until the end of his second term! Well just as I and many retired Generals and Colonels serving in Iraq had called for Rumsfeld's firing, this did not happen prior to the election. However, in this book and other books detailed in my Selected Bibliography, Rumsfeld's resignation was cited. It was demonstrated of Rumsfeld's criminal dereliction of his duties when in April 2003 he and Bremmer disbanded the Iraqi Army. There was a small window in which there may have been a military solution. This detrimental action destroyed the possibility of winning the Iraq War militarily in April 2003. Rumsfeld should have been immediately fired in April 2003, almost 3 ½ years ago! And additionally, it borders on treason, traitor ship that George Tenet and Bremmer received the Medals of Freedom as the Blood of the 3500 who have given all in Iraq are on their hands; and if successful an Emergency Executive Order will be issued on January 20, 2009, immediately revoking and surrendering their Medals of Freedom, and if not returned to the government at once, arrest warrants will be issued for the U.S. Army to take both George Tenet and Bremmer into prison custody!

Now, mid January 2007 Bush is proposing to send over 20,000 more troops to Baghdad, Iraq! It seems that the acting Presidents, "for whom it has seemed that they are Cheney and Rove," are the ones who are calling all the shots! It certainly has been that way for over six years. This administration has never admitted to making any mistakes. And for the past four years "they attacked anyone and everyone who challenged the war and the invading of this sovereign country of Iraq! And now in January 2007, we have in America almost 75% of Americans who realize we cannot win Iraq militarily; there is a civil war in Iraq. Our God-fearing men and women soldiers are shooting targets! The Iraqis have to settle their differences and govern themselves. There is 84% unemployment in Iraq and Baghdad; 85% of the Muslim Sunnis and 84% of the Muslim Shia wish for America to pull our troops out of Iraq. Praise God for the responsible investigative journalism of Newsweek as in their December 4, 2006, issue in their featured article "Moqtada al-Sadr, The Man to See in Iraq," page 26. All Americans should read this article. Praise God that you at Newsweek will continue to keep up the excellent work. This article not only shows the Islam population in the entire Middle East, but it breaks down the Muslim Sunni and Muslim Shite population. It also breaks down the oil production and oil revenues of the entire Middle East. It also shows the United Iraqi Alliance government, and most importantly the controlling parties including Cleric Moqtada al-Sadr of "the Sadrists." What the Bush administration has failed to do for all the six years they have been in office is to open dialogue to all including Palestine, Syria, Iran, Saudia Arabia, and Hezbollah in Lebanon, Moqtda al-Sadr in Iraq and all others. The next President of America must open communication to all in the world. As I previously stated, right now in America we don't seem to have leaders who are really interested in world peace. God is in control! Jesus Christ is the "Prince of Peace!" I worship the "Prince of Peace."

When I traveled around the world in 63 days in 1985, I flew 59,000 air miles. I discovered that even though I only speak two languages, English and Spanish, you still could manage to communicate with other people of other nations. It may take you a little longer to communicate your dialogue to them. My wife is, as mentioned earlier, is a U.S. Naturalized Citizen from the Philippines, and she speaks four languages with English being one of those languages. I do believe God is in Control! One of the items discussed in the Newsweek article was on page 30, was when Saddam Hussein murdered Moqtada al-Sadr's father, Muhammad Sadiq al-Sadr and two of his eldest sons. "But gunman—assumed to be working for Saddam—murdered the elder Sadr along with two of his sons in 1999. Moqtada was 25 at the time." At the memorial service for Moqtada's father and his two brothers, Saddam Hussein tried to bribe Moqtada. He tried to find out what his price was! However, Saddam Hussein found out Moqtada al-Sadr could not be bought!

What I want to convey to all Americans is that this shall not be my last book! This is my first book, but I anticipate there will be sequels. Just as in the past sixteen years, I realize we have a lot of blemished politicians in Washington, D.C. Just as the media reports that it is a cinch, a slam dunk that Hillary Clinton will get the Democratic nomination for President and will probably become the first woman President of America. But her husband is still a fornicator, adulterer still fornicating, adulterating it up with Canadian women and other women around the world as reported by the New York Times recently. Nothing has changed! Again, as stated earlier, when I asked Ms Ruth Pate's Newspapers, Journalism, and Broadcast class of Dorman High School recently the questions "Do you think that a woman could be elected President of America? It was unanimous, "All agreed that there were many millions of American women who are qualified to become the first woman President of America, and Hillary Clinton is not one of those!"

I have been in preliminary negotiations with a God Fearing American woman who would come on board and come walk with us and participate with us in this grass roots movement and campaign across America. Of course, those negotiations have not been finalized, and upon finalization it will be announced in the media and published on our Google web blogger site, colonelsanders2008@blogspot.com Please visit our web site and purchase a copy of this book online at colonelsanders2008@blogspot.com on google blogger. Or you may visit the self publishing website www.lulu.com and purchase a copy from the book store.

Again this book is "Grass Roots Co-President's Campaign; Create 2,500,000 Disciples of America", by me, Colonel Launeil Sanders. Help us in the grass roots God Fearing movement! Buy a copy of my book. Additionally, please visit our web site and sign up as one of the 50,000 disciples from your state to expedite our grass roots movement in achieving our 2,500,000 disciples prior to the January 2008 primary campaigns! May God inspire you for your daily communion with Him to enjoy that only real love, joy, peace, harmony, happiness and the ultimate loving of your neighbors of America. My yahoo email account is colonel_launeilsanders@yahoo.com

If God let's Jesus Christ walk with us on this grass roots political movement "no exceptions as everything is accomplishable" as God says in His word from Philippians 4:10-13 and in the verse 13, "I can do all things through Christ which strengtheneth me"

As Janneth and I are very thankful to God that he has brought many God-fearing Christian brothers and sisters in Christ in our life and as Tony Dale and I were discussing our complete trust in our Almighty Father, Tony shared again the most powerful devotional:

"DIS...OR EN...COURAGEMENT"

"It is so very easy for us to become discouraged. The vagaries of life with unexpected disappointment, pain, and suffering batter against the walls of our lives like hurricane driven waves. We hope and wish for outcomes that never seem to come to fruition. It is then, at the point where the circumstances of our lives seem dire that the true test of our faith is waged. The enemy whispers in our mind words of fear, hopelessness, and regret. He bludgeons our emotions with the weapon of discouragement. Dis – courage – ment. He comes to steal our courage. If he can rob us of our will to hold fast to God's promises, he can weaken our faith and eventually steal our power.

Ah! But we have a source of infinite strength upon which to draw if we but cry out for help. "For in all these things we overwhelmingly conquer through Him who loved us" (Romans 8:37). The verse continues to enumerate all the circumstances and challenges. He will help us to overcome but how are we to access this power? Faith.

We all have faith. The question is what are you putting your faith in? Your strength, your talents, your circumstances, your looks? What is real faith anyway?

"Faith is the <u>assurance</u> of things hoped for, the conviction (evidence) of things not seen"

(Hebrews 11:1). To see how that looks, read the whole chapter, the 'Hall of Heroes' of faith.

Simply put, the antidote to dis-courage-ment is en-courage-ment found in the promises of His word and through prayer and the answers He gives us through it. We must be willing, however, to wait for Him to act, to tough it out, never losing hope or surrendering our faith to discouragement. "Wait for the Lord, be strong and let your heart take courage, yes, wait for the Lord."

We choose how we view the conditions we confront. The choice determines our experience and usefulness in this life. There is a simple formula for applying faith: C + P = E. Circumstance (C) plus Perspective (P) equals Experience (E).

Who are you going to listen to? What lens will you view the circumstances of your life through? Abraham Lincoln said, "A man is as happy or unhappy as he makes up his mind to be." We determine who we heed in our thoughts. Do you choose to entertain doubt, discouragement, fear or hope and certainty that God is working in our best interests?

"For I know the plans that I have for you declares the Lord. Plans for welfare and not calamity to give you a future and hope. Then you will call upon Me and I will listen to you" (Jeremiah 29:11-12)."

SELETED BIBLIOGRAPHY

Ryrie Study BIBLE, King James Version: The Greatest of all BOOKS, by Charles Caldwell Ryrie, Th.D., Ph. D.

Don't Give Up, Don't Ever Give Up: A Young Man's True Story of Tragedy, Patience, and Hope, by Brian Webb

Imperial Life in the Emerald City: Inside Iraq's Green Zone, by Rajiv Chandrasekaran

Out of Iraq: A Political Plan for Withdrawal Now, By George McGovern

Fiasco: The American Military Adventure in Iraq, by Thomas E. Ricks

Cobra II: The Inside Story of the Invasion and Occupation of Iraq, by Michael R. Gordon, Bernard E. Trainor, Thomas E. Ricks

Hubris: The Inside Story of Spin, Scandal, and the Selling of the Iraq War, by David Corn, Michael Isikoff, David Corn

The One Percent Doctrine: Deep Inside America's Pursuit of Its Enemies Since 9/11, by Ron Suskind

The Greatest Story Ever Told: The Decline and Fall of Truth from 9/11 to Katrina, by Frank Rich

State Of Denial: Presents An Insightful Glimpse Into the Inner Workings of the Bush Administration as It Led Our Country Into the war in Iraq, by Bob Woodward

Freedom Writers Diary: How a Teacher and 150 Teens Used Writing to Change Themselves and the World, by The Freedom Writers, Erin Gruwell, Erin Gruwell (With), Zlata Filipovic

The Daily Show with Jon Stewart Presents America (The Book): A Citizen's Guide to Democracy Inaction, by Jon Stewart

90 Minutes in Heaven: A True Story of Death and Life, by Don Piper

Flags of Our Fathers: Raising the flag at Iwo Jima, by James Bradley, Ron Powers

The Innocent Man: Book Concerns a Man Sentenced to Death for a Crime He Did Not Commit, And Since Grisham is a Former Lawyer Presents More Proof of America's Totally Broken Legal System, by John Grisham

The Way to Win: Clinton,Bush, Rove, and How to Take the White House in 2008, by Mark Halperin, John F. Harris

Being Still And Knowing: The Power of Christian Intimacy in Which Author, Tony Dale, Speaks of God's Showering of His Blessings on Those Who Worship and Obey Him, by Tony Dale

The Political Zoo: Radio Commentator Michael Savage likens America's political scene to a zoo , by Michael Savage

Team of Rivals: The Political Genius of Abraham Lincoln, by Doris Kearns Goodwin

American Theocracy: The Peril and Politics of Radical Religion, Oil, and Borrowed Money in the 21st Century, by Kevin Phillips

American at the Crossroads: Democracy, Power, and the Neoconservative Legacy, by Francis Fukuyama

The Politics of Jesus: Rediscovering the True Revolutionary Nature of Jesus' Teachings and How They Have Been Corrupted, by Obery M. Hendricks

Mayflower: A story of Courage, Community, and War, by Nathaniel Philbrick, Edward Herrmann (Narrated by), Edward Herrmann (Read by)

<u>The Quest For Authentic Manhood</u>: Sets Out To Answer Some Questions That Are Universal To Men, by Dr. Robert Lewis

<u>Chasing Ghosts</u>: , A Soldier's Fight for America from Baghdad to Washington, by Paul Reickhoff, Iraq Veteran

PHOTOGRAPHS, GRAPHICS

Page 17, Photograph 1, Natalie Caroline Sanders and Aaron Neil Sanders, our two biological children God granted Evelyn and me

Page 18, Photograph 2- Son Aaron Sanders and his wife Allison; Bottom photo, from left Janneth Sanders, Aaron Sanders, wife Allison holding our daughter Dorothy Love Sanders

Page 19, Photograph 3 -From left, wife Evelyn, stepson Ronnie Franklin, Launeil, Natalie in Evelyn's lap and Aaron in insert

Page 38, Photograph 4, Janneth in her blue dress;

Page 36 and 37, Graphics 5, Janneth's Love is Priceless letter mailed to me from her in Philippines.

Page 44, Photograph 6, formal tux photos of Launeil I mailed to Janneth.

Page 50 , Photograph 7, husband, Launeil Sanders, and wife, Janneth Sanders, in wedding toast;

Page 51, Photograph 8, Launeil Sanders and Janneth Emberador Sanders, husband and wife down the aisle after pronounced Husband and Wife in God's Holy Matrimony Ceremony of God's Marriage;

Page 52, Photograph 9, Launeil Sanders and Janneth Emberador Sanders, husband and wife cutting the cake

Page 53, Photograph 10, Launeil Sanders feeding Janneth Emberador Sanders a piece of the cake;

Page 54, Photograph 11, group wedding photo of Janneth and Launeil with my sister, Janice Harden to right of Janneth and best man, my brother, George Larry Sanders, to left of me;

Page 55, Photograph 12, Launeil Sanders and Janneth Emberador Sanders, with full view of our cake baked by the God- Fearing American Ann Harber;

Page 56, Photograph 13, Friends of Launeil and Janneth at reception including top photo, Floyd Craig back to camera, from left of Floyd, Pastor Tracy, Margaret Craig, Ed Cartwright and Betty Cartwright, Harold Craig, Ann Harber, Floyd's daughter and Floyd's wife. Bottom photo, Mickey Criag and sister's husband Troy Harden and at second table above brother, Larry Sanders, and my aunt, Joan Sanders;

Page 57, Photograph 14, group wedding photo of Janneth and Launeil, from the left, step father, Harold Craig, my Mother, Dorothy Craig, my sister, Janice Harden, Janneth, Launeil and my best man, my brother, George Larry Sanders, to left of me.

Page 65, Photograph 15, which has two photos with first top of Launeil and Janneth on skiis during one of our honeymoon trips to Telluride ski resort at Telluride, Colorado, and the bottom photo of one of us on our bikes at our home in Spartanburg.

Page 66, Photograph 16, consists of three skiing photos of Janneth on our honeymoon in Telluride resort.

Page 67, Photograph 17, consists of top photo, of Mother and Janneth behind their motorhome at Mountain View. The bottom photo shows me and Janneth, Harold with his back to camera, and Martha and her husband in background.

Page 68, Photograph 18, consists of top photo, with from left Harold Craig, Betty Cartwright, her husband Ed Cartwright sitting with his guitar, Janneth, Mother, and Floyd Craig. The middle photo, shows Janneth and Ed Cartwright. The bottom photo consists of many friends of Harold and Mother with Janneth and includes Ed and Betty Cartwright, Martha and her husband Walter, Floyd Craig and others.

Page 72, Photograph 19, which shows from left Juanita Emberador, her Mother, Antonio Emberador, Janneth's Father, Janneth and Dorothy Love in center.

Page 73, Photograph 20, which consists of three photos: the top photos shows from left Janneth, Pastor Deese's wife and another sister in Christ. The middle photo shows Janneth opening presents and Assistant Pastor's wife Pat holding Dorothy Love; and the bottom photo shows from left Janneth, Mrs Smith, Pastor Deese's wife and another sister in Christ.

Page 77, Photograph 21, which shows my biological Mother and father, Dorothy Love Sanders and Aaron Sanders Jr.

Page 90, Photograph 23, consists of the following: top photo, from left Langiene , Thien Pham's daughter, Dorothy Love and David, Thien Pham's son; middle photo from left, Thien Pham , Langiene, Launeil, David, and Thien Pham's wife Naw and Dorothy Love in high chair. Bottom photo consists from left Naw , Dorothy Love, Langiene and Janneth.

Page 91, Photograph 22, consists of the following: top photo, from left Mrs. Emma Mackey in pink coat holding Dorothy Love's hand, back row Kimberly Mack, Mary Mack, Launeil, Deacon Tony Jones and Tony Jones' son. Bottom photo, shows Mrs. Emma Mackey holding Dorothy Love's hand.

Page 98, Photograph 24, which consists of the following: from left their adopted daughter from Philippines, Andy's wife Jenny, Andy Bartley and with Andy holding his and Jenny's son, Corbin.

Page103, Photograph 25, which is our son, Colonel Tony Sanders, pinching Winnie The Pooh's nose!

Page 104, Photograph 26, Colonel Tony Sanders, at approximately three years old.

Page 106, Photograph 27, Colonel Tony Sanders, riding and driving his red fire engine.

Page106, Photograph 28, Colonel Sanders and Dorothy Love Sanders (with her on her knees) holding hands

Page 107, Photograph 29, Colonel Tony Sanders sitting on his red stool

Page 108, Photograph 30, Dorothy Love Sanders with her hands on Colonel Tony Sanders' shoulders.

Page 109, Photograph 31, Dorothy Love Sanders at two weeks old in her red dress and Colonel Tony Sanders' at a few weeks old in his blue 45 jump suit

Page 110, Photograph 32, Launeil in Tux standing with Dorothy Love Sanders with the American Flag and balloons!

Page 111, Photograph 33, Launeil with holding Colonel Tony Sanders' in my lap

Page 149, Photograph 44, Janneth's U.S. Naturalization Ceremony at the U.S. Federal Courthouse in Greenville, South Carolina. In this photo from left, her sister Tonnette Williams, Janneth sitting, Launeil and Dorothy Love

Page 150, Photograph 45, Janneth's U.S. Naturalization Ceremony at the U.S. Federal Courthouse in Greenville, South Carolina. In this first top photo from left, Janneth, Dorothy Love in middle, and Launeil. Bottom photo, her sister Tonnette Williams, and Janneth.

Page 157, Photograph 46, President Bush with his hands on the shoulders of our daughter, Dorothy Love Sanders.

Page 158, Photograph 47, Honorable U.S. Senator John McCain and 2000 Presidential Candidate shaking hands with our daughter, Dorothy Love Sanders.

Page 170, Photograph 48, Janneth inside red Austin Healey with Mother looking on.

Page 171, Photograph 49, Mother, Launeil, Dorothy Love and Janneth at her home in Atoka, Tennessee.

Page 172, Photograph 50, Mother sitting outside at her house in Atoka, Tennessee, opening presents at her 73 rd birthday in October 1993. Bottom photo is another photo of Mother holding Dorothy Love.

Page 173, Photograph 51, Mother sitting on her sofa holding Dorothy Love at her home in Memphis, Tennessee. The middle photo from left has Launeil, Dorothy Love in the red wagon and Mother on right. The bottom photo has another photo of Mother with Dorothy Love on her couch together.

Page 39, Photograph 52, which is the first photo that Janneth sent me in January 1993 in her yellow dress and hat outfit.

INDEX

A

B

C

D

E

F

G

H

M

N

O

P

Q

R

S

T

U

X

Y

Z

www.ingramcontent.com/pod-product-compliance
Lightning Source LLC
Chambersburg PA
CBHW081346280326
41927CB00042B/3122